EMBRACING THE FEMME FATALE

UNLEASHING YOUR INNER POWER AND CHARISMA

BY

EMILY SAMANTHA

"Embracing the Femme Fatale: Unleashing Your Inner Power and Charisma" is a book with a distinct purpose - to guide women on their journey towards self-empowerment and personal mastery. It serves as a roadmap for readers to embrace their individuality, develop their unique charisma, and understand the allure of the Femme Fatale archetype. Through this exploration, the book fosters a deep sense of self-discovery and personal growth. It provides practical strategies and actionable insights to improve communication skills, emotional intelligence, and resilience, underlining a comprehensive approach to personal development that considers mental, emotional, and physical well-being.

Moreover, it delivers invaluable advice on navigating complex personal and professional relationships, striking a balance between respect, understanding, and maintaining healthy boundaries. This involves an insightful exploration of power dynamics, attraction, and the nuanced art of seduction. Crucially, the book challenges and dismantles common stereotypes and misconceptions associated with Femme Fatales, urging readers to redefine the archetype in a positive and empowering light.

Emphasizing the uniqueness of each individual's journey, the book encourages women to carve their own path as a Femme Fatale, celebrating the diversity and individuality inherent in this process. In summary, "Embracing the Femme Fatale: Unleashing Your Inner Power and Charisma" is an empowering guide for any woman keen to harness her inner power, steer relationships with confidence, and live life authentically and unapologetically on her own terms.

TABLE OF CONTENTS

CHAPTER 1

INTRODUCTION

Femme Fatale," originating from French, translates to "Fatal Woman" in English. This captivating archetype has intrigued and delighted audiences for centuries, finding roots in ancient mythology, seeping into literature, and eventually taking a prominent place in cinema and popular culture. However, defining a Femme Fatale as a dangerously attractive woman would oversimplify a complex character filled with intriguing dichotomies and potent symbolism.

A Femme Fatale embodies a blend of seductiveness, cunning, power, and mystery. She's often portrayed as a woman who uses charm and wit to achieve her objectives, ranging from personal survival to revenge, ambition, or even love. The essence of the Femme Fatale lies in her subversion of traditional gender roles and her assertive, often intimidating independence.

However, the Femme Fatale is not merely a predatory figure. This archetype frequently symbolizes a rebellion against societal norms and expectations. Her audacity, self-reliance, and unapologetic pursuit of her desires challenge the traditional notion of femininity. Yet, her allure is indisputable, with her charisma creating an irresistible magnetism that draws people towards her, regardless of the danger that might accompany her.

But it's worth noting that the concept of a Femme Fatale is neither one-dimensional nor stagnant; it has evolved. Earlier portrayals often depicted Femme Fatales as villainous or morally ambiguous figures who met tragic ends—perhaps a reflection of society's discomfort with powerful women. Over time, however, this portrayal has changed. The modern Femme Fatale is often represented as a woman who commands her destiny, a figure of empowerment rather than one of treachery or danger.

Today's Femme Fatale symbolizes strength, resilience, and confidence. She leverages her intelligence and charisma to navigate a world that often seeks to limit her. Her allure lies not just in her physical attractiveness but, more significantly, in her self-assured demeanor, quick wit, and emotional intelligence. She is not afraid to express her desires or pursue her goals, and she does so with captivating sophistication and elegance.

However, embracing the Femme Fatale archetype doesn't imply manipulating others or acting unethically. The Femme Fatale's true power lies in her emotional autonomy and ability to assert herself in personal and professional arenas. Being a Femme Fatale is about understanding and owning one's identity, desires, and skills and using them to navigate the world confidently and gracefully.

That anyone can embrace the essence of a Femme Fatale is not about embodying an archetype as it is portrayed in movies or books. It's about interpreting and representing the aspects that resonate with and empower you. Maybe the Femme Fatale's confidence appeals to you, or perhaps her resilience or independence. Whatever the case, the Femme Fatale concept is a powerful tool to explore one's potential, break free from societal limitations, and take control of one's destiny.

Understanding the concept of "Femme Fatale" is about exploring this wealthy, historical figure filled with dichotomies and contradictions. It's about understanding the Femme Fatale's place in culture, evolution over time, and relevance in the modern world. More than anything, it's about realizing that the Femme Fatale symbolizes a potent form of feminine power and individuality. Embracing the Femme Fatale within is not about becoming someone else; it's about unleashing your strength, charisma, and energy and becoming the best version of yourself.

Debunking myths and misconceptions

As with many archetypes, the Femme Fatale has been encrusted with many myths and misconceptions that must be dispelled. These distortions often stem from cultural stereotypes, partial portrayals in media, and societal unease with female autonomy and power.

One common myth is the portrayal of the Femme Fatale as a villainous figure. Historically, she has often been cast as the antagonist who brings about the downfall of the protagonists, usually men, in narratives. However, this view must be revised and accurately capture the Femme Fatale archetype's breadth. While the Femme Fatale can be a disruptive force, it's worth noting that her 'disruptions' often stem from rejecting societal norms and expectations, particularly those that restrict her autonomy. She is not inherently evil but is a complex character, capable of both kindness and cruelty, depending on her circumstances and goals.

Another widely held misconception is that a Femme Fatale is defined by her physical attractiveness alone. This perspective is reductive and overlooks her more nuanced characteristics. The allure of a Femme Fatale certainly encompasses physical beauty, but it also includes intelligence, wit, charisma, and emotional strength. She is a multidimensional character whose appeal lies as much in her mind as her appearance.

It's also a myth that a Femme Fatale uses manipulation and deceit as her primary tools. This belief stems from a selective interpretation of her actions. While a Femme Fatale can employ manipulation, it's essential to understand that she operates within a society that often tries to limit her power and choices. However, the modern interpretation of the Femme Fatale emphasizes emotional intelligence, self-confidence, and assertiveness as her defining traits rather than deceit.

A particularly detrimental misconception is that the Femme Fatale is an emblem of female 'dangerousness' or 'immorality.' This view has roots in patriarchal societal structures where powerful, autonomous women are often seen as threatening. In contrast, the Femme Fatale should be seen as an embodiment of female empowerment—a woman who asserts her desires seeks her path, and refuses to be boxed into societal norms.

A further myth is that all Femme Fatales are the same. This perception results in a one-dimensional view of this multifaceted archetype. Femme Fatales is diverse, with varied goals, characteristics, and approaches. What unites them is their assertion of individuality, refusal to be passive players in their lives, and ability to assert their will against the odds.

Lastly, the notion that only a specific 'type' of woman can embody the Femme Fatale archetype is a myth. Femme Fatales come from all walks of life, incorporating various personalities, appearances, and backgrounds. The power of the Femme Fatale lies in her autonomy, resilience, and individuality—not specific physical attributes or a singular personality type.

In debunking these myths, we free the Femme Fatale from restrictive stereotypes and appreciate her as an empowering figure. She becomes an emblem of courage, resilience, and individuality. By seeing past the misconceptions, we can understand the Femme Fatale as a celebration of women who challenge norms, assert their identity, and command their destinies. The true Femme Fatale is not a threat but a beacon, shining a light on the power of autonomy, the beauty of complexity, and the potential within us all.

"Embracing the Femme Fatale: Unleashing Your Inner Power and Charisma" is a transformative guide designed to navigate readers on a path of self-discovery and personal empowerment. The central goal of this book is to deconstruct and understand the Femme Fatale archetype in a modern, positive, and empowering light and guide readers in embodying this concept to enhance their lives.

The book's first part serves as an introduction to the Femme Fatale, exploring her historical roots, evolution, and significance in contemporary society. This section serves as a foundation for the reader's understanding, providing context and creating a comprehensive picture of this multifaceted archetype.

Next, the book delves into a detailed exploration of the Femme Fatale's defining traits—her assertiveness, emotional intelligence, resilience, and unique charm. This section elucidates these characteristics using illustrative examples and scientific studies, offering readers the tools to integrate these attributes into their own lives.

Much of the book debunks common myths and misconceptions about the Femme Fatale. By dispelling these misinterpretations, the book helps readers shed any negative or restrictive beliefs about this archetype and view the Femme Fatale as an empowering and positive figure.

The book then transitions to a more practical and interactive segment, guiding readers through actionable steps to embrace the Femme Fatale within themselves. This includes exercises for building self-confidence, developing emotional intelligence, improving communication skills, and fostering resilience. Each of these steps is designed to help the readers identify, nurture, and express their inner Femme Fatale in ways that resonate with their identities.

Towards the end, the book guides how to navigate relationships as a modern Femme Fatale, emphasizing mutual respect, understanding, and maintaining healthy boundaries. It offers insights into handling power dynamics, attraction, and even confrontation in various relationships, equipping the readers to navigate their social world with grace, confidence, and wisdom.

The book concludes by encouraging individuality, emphasizing that there is no single 'right' way to be a Femme Fatale. It champions diversity and personal interpretation of the Femme Fatale archetype, encouraging readers to create unique versions of a Femme Fatale that reflect their strengths, values, and aspirations.

Through this structure, "Embracing the Femme Fatale: Unleashing Your Inner Power and Charisma" is an enlightening resource on the Femme Fatale archetype and a practical manual for personal development. It aims to inspire readers to channel the Femme Fatale's empowering aspects, enhancing their self-confidence, autonomy, and resilience and ultimately enabling them to live more fulfilling, authentic lives.

CHAPTER 2

HISTORICAL CONTEXT OF FEMME FATALES

The origins of the Femme Fatale archetype trace back to ancient civilizations and mythologies, where she took the form of goddesses, queens, and other powerful women. From the captivating Cleopatra to the enchanting Sirens of Greek mythology and the seductive yet deadly biblical figure of Lilith, her presence is notable across various cultures and epochs. These early incarnations were often characterized by their irresistible allure, independent spirit, and the peril they posed to men. These qualities became the foundational traits of the Femme Fatale.

During the Middle Ages, as societal norms became more rigid and patriarchal, the Femme Fatale was depicted as an embodiment of sin, danger, and seduction, often facing tragic ends. Such portrayals can be seen in literature, where characters like Morgan le Fay from Arthurian legends used their beauty and wiles to manipulate and bring ruin.

In the 19th and early 20th centuries, the figure of the Femme Fatale flourished in art and literature. As society underwent significant changes, the Femme Fatale symbolized the fear and fascination surrounding the emerging 'New Woman'—the independent, liberated woman seeking equality and rights. Iconic literary figures like Oscar Wilde's Salome or Gustave Flaubert's Emma Bovary highlighted this tension, embodying the alluring yet threatening female figure who rebelled against societal norms.

However, the film industry, particularly Film Noir of the 1940s and 1950s, solidified the modern image of the Femme Fatale. Characters like Barbara Stanwyck's Phyllis Dietrichson in "Double Indemnity" or Rita Hayworth's Gilda became symbolic of the Femme Fatale—seductive, cunning, and unafraid to use their appeal to get what they wanted.

Yet, as society evolved, so did the portrayal of the Femme Fatale. The late 20th and early 21st centuries saw a shift toward a more empowering representation of the Femme Fatale. Today, she is often seen as a woman in control of her destiny, unapologetically pursuing her desires and using her intelligence and charisma as much as her physical appeal. She is no longer a figure of moral caution but a symbol of female power, autonomy, and resilience. Characters like Amy Dunne in "Gone Girl" or Villanelle in "Killing Eve" exemplify this modern interpretation.

Throughout her evolution, the Femme Fatale has reflected society's anxieties, fascinations, and evolving views about female power and sexuality. She has transitioned from a figure of caution to a symbol of empowerment, encapsulating the struggle and triumph of female autonomy. This rich historical journey makes understanding the Femme Fatale fascinating and essential as we continue to explore and redefine gender norms and roles in our society.

Prominent Femme Fatales in history and their influence
Over centuries, numerous prominent Femme Fatales have left indelible impressions on society and culture. Their influence has shaped perceptions of femininity, power, and allure, challenging norms and reshaping narratives.

Cleopatra: As the last active ruler of Egypt's Ptolemaic Kingdom, Cleopatra is one of the earliest historical figures embodying the Femme Fatale archetype. Her legendary beauty, charm, and intellect are said to have enticed powerful men like Julius Caesar and Mark Antony. Cleopatra was not merely a seductress; she was a powerful ruler and diplomat, her influence extending far beyond her legendary love affairs. She has remained a symbol of allure, power, and resourcefulness throughout history.

Mata Hari: An exotic dancer and courtesan turned World War I spy, Mata Hari remains a notorious Femme Fatale of the 20th century. Despite being executed for espionage, her image as a captivating and dangerous woman who used her seductive skills for intelligence has persisted in popular culture, symbolizing the interplay between attraction, deceit, and power.

Marilyn Monroe: A Hollywood icon, Monroe played up her sex appeal and used it to her advantage in her career, embodying the glamour and allure associated with the Femme Fatale. However, her vulnerability and tragic end have also contributed to a more nuanced perception of the Femme Fatale, highlighting the pressures and pitfalls of such a persona in a male-dominated society.

In literature and film

Lady Macbeth: One of the earliest literary Femme Fatales, Lady Macbeth from Shakespeare's "Macbeth," uses her influence over her husband to spur him into committing regicide. Her ambition, manipulation, and eventual descent into madness create a complex and powerful Femme Fatale figure that has intrigued audiences for centuries.

Scarlett O'Hara: The protagonist of Margaret Mitchell's "Gone with the Wind," Scarlett embodies the strength, resilience, and determination of a Femme Fatale. Her relentless pursuit of what she wants, regardless of societal norms and expectations, redefined the archetype for a new era.

Catwoman: In the world of comic books, Catwoman, aka Selina Kyle, is a notable Femme Fatale. Her complex relationship with Batman, her moral ambiguity, and her combination of sensuality and physical prowess make her a powerful contemporary incarnation of the Femme Fatale.

These influential figures have contributed to the evolution and interpretation of the Femme Fatale archetype. Through their stories, they've challenged societal norms and expectations about women's roles, proving that women can wield power, assert their autonomy, and follow their desires, reflecting the shifting dynamics of gender, energy, and society.

CHAPTER 3

THE FEMME FATALE MINDSET

Embracing the archetype of the Femme Fatale is as much a personal journey as it is a societal statement. At the heart of this journey lies the cultivation of self-confidence and resilience – attributes critical to asserting individuality and navigating life's challenges. Let's explore how we can foster these traits to harness our inner Femme Fatale.

Self-confidence is fundamentally a belief in oneself and one's abilities. This assuredness allows the Femme Fatale to assert her desires and make her choices without second-guessing herself or being swayed by external opinions. Building self-confidence starts with self-awareness – identifying your strengths, weaknesses, values, and passions. We can appreciate our worth and potential when we truly understand and accept ourselves. Take time to recognize your achievements, no matter how small, and use them to reinforce your belief in your capabilities. Regularly practicing self-affirmation and visualization can also enhance self-confidence. However, remember that it's okay to have self-doubt; it's about not letting those moments define you.

Meanwhile, resilience refers to our ability to bounce back from setbacks and adversity. The quality allows the Femme Fatale to face challenges and obstacles head-on, never allowing them to deter her from her path. To build resilience, we must first adopt a positive mindset – viewing challenges as opportunities for growth rather than insurmountable obstacles. Maintain a problem-solving attitude, focusing on possible solutions rather than dwelling on the problem. Developing strong support networks comprising people who inspire and uplift you can also bolster your resilience. Remember, strength isn't about falling but about always getting back up.

Moreover, self-confidence and resilience often go hand in hand – as our self-confidence grows, so does our strength, and vice versa. As we face and overcome challenges, we gain confidence in our ability to handle adversity. Similarly, as we grow more confident in our capabilities, we become better equipped to tackle the obstacles that come our way.

Cultivating these traits is a continuous process that requires patience, dedication, and self-compassion. But by fostering self-confidence and resilience, we not only draw closer to embodying the Femme Fatale archetype but also equip ourselves with essential life skills that enhance our overall well-being and success. As we nurture these qualities, we discover our strength and potential and, in doing so, unleash our inner Femme Fatale – a woman who is self-assured, resilient, and unafraid to embrace her power and charm.

Developing a solid sense of self and individuality

A distinguishing aspect of the Femme Fatale archetype is her strong sense of self and individuality. This character is not defined by societal norms or expectations but by her authentic self. Cultivating this strong sense of self and identity is crucial to channel your inner Femme Fatale.

Self-discovery is the first step in this process. It involves exploring your passions, values, strengths, weaknesses, beliefs, and aspirations. This exploration helps you understand who you are, independent of societal roles and expectations. A range of reflective activities like journaling, meditation, and mindful contemplation can facilitate this self-discovery process.

Once you clearly understand who you are, the next step is self-acceptance. This means acknowledging and accepting your whole self, including your flaws and vulnerabilities. Understand that everyone has strengths and weaknesses; what matters is how you embrace them. This acceptance paves the way for self-love, fostering a healthy relationship with yourself.

Having established this strong self-connection, you can then express your individuality. This involves asserting your unique traits, perspectives, and style, regardless of societal standards or norms. It's about making choices that align with your values and desires, not because others expect or accept them. Your individuality is your unique imprint, and expressing it allows you to live authentically.

Asserting your individuality also involves:

- Setting boundaries.
- Communicating your needs and wants.
- Standing up for yourself when necessary.

It's about proactively shaping your life and relationships to honor your individuality.

However, developing a solid sense of self and individuality is not a one-time event but an ongoing journey of self-discovery, acceptance, and expression. It requires courage, self-compassion, and patience, as you'll need to confront aspects of yourself that you might have previously ignored or denied. But this journey is enriching, empowering you to live more authentically and passionately.

By cultivating a strong sense of self and individuality, you embody the spirit of the Femme Fatale - a woman who knows herself, accepts herself, expresses herself, and lives life on her terms. And in doing so, you become more self-assured and satisfied with life and inspire others to embrace their individuality and authenticity.

Embracing independence and empowerment

A core component of the Femme Fatale archetype is her profound sense of independence and empowerment. This trait isn't merely about being self-sufficient; it's about confidently asserting oneself, making autonomous decisions, and taking charge of one's life.

To cultivate independence, begin by gaining self-sufficiency in various aspects of life. This can mean learning new skills, expanding your knowledge, and being able to provide for your basic needs. However, independence goes beyond mere practicality. It's also about emotional self-sufficiency:

- Being comfortable with solitude
- Managing your emotions
- Not relying excessively on others for validation or happiness

Embrace a mindset of growth and continuous learning. Be open to new experiences and challenges, as they offer personal growth and self-discovery opportunities. An independent individual is willing to step outside of their comfort zone.

Making independent decisions is another vital aspect of this journey. Trust your judgment and abilities, and have the courage to make decisions based on your intuition and understanding. It's okay to seek advice and opinions, but the final decision should align with your beliefs and needs.

Independence is closely tied to empowerment, which involves recognizing and asserting your power. License is not about dominating others but controlling your life and standing up for your rights and beliefs. It's about knowing your worth, setting boundaries, and advocating for yourself.

Fostering a sense of empowerment begins with self-respect. Recognize your inherent value and treat yourself with kindness and compassion. Stand up for your rights and needs in your personal and professional life. Practice assertive communication, expressing your thoughts and feelings openly and respectfully.

Also, invest time and energy in nurturing your passions and talents. Success and mastery in areas you love bring fulfillment and enhance your sense of self-efficacy and empowerment.

Finally, surround yourself with positive, supportive individuals who respect and encourage your independence and empowerment. Avoid people and environments that undermine your self-esteem or autonomy.

Embracing independence and empowerment is a transformative journey that aligns you with the spirit of the Femme Fatale and enriches your life. As you become more independent and empowered, you will find yourself living more authentically, confidently, and passionately, embodying the very essence of the Femme Fatale: a woman who is unapologetically herself, in charge of her life, and free to pursue her desires.

CHAPTER 4

PHYSICAL ATTRIBUTES OF A FEMME FATALE

In embodying the archetype of the Femme Fatale, an essential element is cultivating personal style and aesthetics. This isn't about conforming to specific fashion trends or beauty standards but developing a unique visual identity that reflects individuality and personality. This aesthetic isn't purely external; it's a manifestation of your inner self, enhancing your confidence and charisma, integral to the aura of a Femme Fatale.

At its core, personal style is a form of self-expression. It's a non-verbal communication tool that conveys information about who you are and what you stand for. It can reflect your mood, personality, values, and tastes. It can also influence how you feel about yourself and how others perceive you. Being comfortable with your personal style naturally boosts your self-confidence, making you feel more authentic and empowered.

Developing personal style begins with self-awareness. Understand your body, preferences, lifestyle, and comfort level. Do you gravitate toward minimalistic styles or ornate designs? Do you prefer neutral shades or vibrant colors? Do you feel comfortable in fitted clothing or choose a more relaxed fit? Answers to such questions lay the foundation for your style.

Once you've identified your preferences, experiment with different styles, items, and aesthetics to discover what works best for you. Feel free to mix and match. Play with colors, textures, and patterns. Fashion is as much an art form as practicality, and personal style is your unique canvas.

Remember, personal style is not static; it evolves with you. Your style may transform as you grow and change, reflecting your evolving identity and experiences. And that's okay. The aim is not to stick with one type forever but to always feel comfortable and authentic in what you wear.

In addition to clothing, personal style extends to your overall aesthetic, including your grooming, makeup, hairstyle, accessories, and even your living and working spaces. These elements contribute to your visual narrative, shaping your image and the aura you project.

For the Femme Fatale, personal style is a significant aspect of her charm and power. Her aesthetic reflects her confidence, individuality, and autonomy, whether it's the classic glamour of a Film Noir Femme Fatale or the edgy chic of a modern interpretation. It's a tool of empowerment, a statement of her identity, and a celebration of her femininity.

Therefore, personal style's importance lies in its capacity to enhance self-confidence, assert individuality, and express personality. It's about creating a visual identity that resonates with who you are and who you aspire to be. So, as you embark on your journey to unleash your inner Femme Fatale, embrace the process of crafting your unique personal style, and let your aesthetic be a testament to your power, charm, and individuality.

Emphasizing health and wellness over unrealistic beauty standards

In the quest to embrace the essence of the Femme Fatale, it's essential to understand that the true allure of this archetype comes from her inner strength, confidence, and individuality, not merely physical attractiveness as dictated by society's often unrealistic beauty standards. This journey should highlight the importance of health and wellness over these standards, focusing on nurturing your body, mind, and spirit to encourage self-love, respect, and authenticity.

To start, let's address the concept of beauty standards. Throughout history and across cultures, the definition of beauty has been ever-changing, influenced by societal norms, media, and various industries. These standards often promote a single, narrow ideal of beauty, which can lead to harmful comparisons, self-esteem issues, and unhealthy behaviors in pursuit of this ideal.

However, the true essence of beauty lies in diversity and individuality. Everyone has unique physical traits that make them stand out, and these differences should be celebrated, not shunned. Moreover, physical beauty is just one aspect of a person's appeal. Qualities such as kindness, confidence, intelligence, and resilience are equally, if not more, attractive.

Thus, the first step is to shift your perception of beauty. Start by recognizing and challenging any internalized unrealistic beauty standards. Celebrate your unique physical attributes, and focus on enhancing your natural beauty rather than altering your appearance to fit a specific mold.

Secondly, prioritize health and wellness over physical appearance. This involves adopting a balanced diet, regular exercise regime, and sufficient rest, not for weight loss or body shaping, but to nourish and care for your body. When you feel good physically, it naturally enhances your confidence and mood. Moreover, practicing mindfulness, meditation, and other mental health practices can foster emotional well-being.

Self-care is another crucial aspect of health and wellness. This goes beyond skincare or spa days. It means doing what makes you happy and relaxed, whether reading a book, spending time in nature, or catching up with friends. It's about treating yourself with kindness and compassion.

Emphasizing health and wellness also extends to mental and emotional well-being. Cultivate a positive mindset and resilience, foster healthy relationships, and seek professional help when needed. Maintaining a high level of life and overall wellness requires good mental health care.

Lastly, cultivate body positivity and self-love. Embrace your body, with its strengths and imperfections, and appreciate its functionality rather than appearance. Remember to treat your body with compassion and respect and that your appearance does not determine your value.

In embracing the Femme Fatale archetype, remember that her true power lies in her self-confidence, resilience, and individuality, not in adhering to societal beauty standards. By emphasizing health and wellness, you enhance your physical, emotional, and mental well-being and cultivate self-love and body positivity. This approach empowers you to embody the true essence of the Femme Fatale – a woman who is confident, healthy, and unapologetically herself.

CHAPTER 5

MASTERING COMMUNICATION

An integral aspect of the Femme Fatale archetype is her knack for persuasive and effective communication. This doesn't mean manipulation or deceit but the ability to articulate ideas clearly, confidently, and convincingly. The ability to communicate effectively plays a critical role in personal and professional relationships and can significantly enhance your influence and charisma.

Persuasive communication begins with clarity. To convey your thoughts and ideas effectively, you must be clear about what you want to communicate. This requires self-awareness and introspection. Understand your message and its purpose, then tailor it to your audience and context.

Active listening is another critical element of effective communication. It's not just about expressing your thoughts but also understanding others. Listening attentively, asking insightful questions, and showing empathy can foster mutual understanding and trust, enhancing the effectiveness of your communication.

Non-verbal communication also plays a crucial role. Your message may be received more or less effectively depending on your body language, tone of voice, facial expressions, and eye contact. Positive body language, like maintaining eye contact and adopting an open posture, can enhance credibility and approachability.

Persuasive communication also involves the strategic use of rhetoric. This includes using compelling language, storytelling, metaphors, and analogies to make your message more engaging and convincing. Emotional intelligence, understanding your audience's needs, emotions, and perspectives, can significantly enhance your persuasive abilities.

Moreover, assertiveness is a vital aspect of effective communication. It's about expressing your thoughts, feelings, and needs honestly and respectfully without infringing on others' rights. Assertiveness also involves setting boundaries, saying no when necessary, and standing up for yourself.

Finally, effective communication is a two-way process. It involves not only speaking but also listening, observing, and responding. This procedure involves both giving and receiving feedback, which is essential. It helps you understand the impact of your communication and make necessary adjustments.

In embodying the Femme Fatale, mastering the art of persuasive and effective communication is crucial. It enhances your personal and professional relationships, bolsters your influence, and empowers you to express yourself confidently and authentically. By honing these skills, you align yourself with the Femme Fatale spirit - a woman who knows her mind voices her thoughts, and commands attention with her eloquence and charisma.

Understanding and leveraging the power of body language

Body language is a powerful tool in the arsenal of the Femme Fatale archetype. Often speaking louder than words, our gestures, posture, and facial expressions communicate a plethora of information about our feelings, intentions, and confidence.

Understanding and leveraging the power of body language can significantly enhance your personal and professional interactions, making you more persuasive, approachable, and charismatic.

Non-verbal cues account for a substantial portion of our communication, and understanding this unspoken language provides insights into others' thoughts and feelings, making us more empathetic and intuitive communicators. But more importantly, being conscious of our body language helps us project the image we want to portray, whether confidence, interest, openness, or assertiveness.

Posture is a critical element of body language. Standing tall with your shoulders back conveys confidence and assertiveness. On the other hand, slouching or shrinking can make you seem unsure or uninterested. Emulating the Femme Fatale means owning your space, standing tall and firm, and showcasing your inner strength and confidence.

Eye contact is another critical aspect. It communicates attentiveness, respect, and sincerity. Maintaining steady but comfortable eye contact during conversations enhances your credibility and indicates your engagement and interest in the exchange.

Facial expressions also convey a wealth of information. A genuine smile can make you seem more approachable and friendly. Raising eyebrows can express surprise or skepticism while furrowing them can signify concentration or confusion. Matching your facial expressions to your verbal message strengthens the impact of your communication.

Hand gestures, too, can enhance your expressiveness. They can emphasize points, convey enthusiasm, or express certain emotions. However, it's essential to ensure these gestures are controlled and deliberate, not fidgety or nervous.

Mirroring, subtly reflecting someone else's body language, can create rapport and empathy in interactions. However, it should be done subtly and appropriately to avoid seeming insincere or manipulative.

Understanding cultural differences in body language is also vital. Certain gestures might be considered polite in one culture but offensive in another. Awareness of such differences is crucial, especially in multicultural or international contexts.

Leveraging the power of body language requires practice and mindfulness. It's about becoming aware of your non-verbal cues and intentionally using them to enhance communication. As you master this skill, you'll become more influential and charismatic, echoing the Femme Fatale's allure.

Body language isn't about performing; it's about projecting your authentic self. It's about embodying the Femme Fatale's confidence and assertiveness in every aspect of your demeanor, creating a powerful and lasting impression. By harnessing the power of body language, you can communicate more effectively, enhance your relationships, and command attention, just like a true Femme Fatale.

The role of mystery and subtly in communication

For a Femme Fatale, mastering the art of communication involves more than just verbal and non-verbal cues. It also consists in harnessing the power of mystery and subtlety. By not revealing everything at once and leaving some things to the imagination, you invite intrigue and fascination, creating a sense of allure and magnetism synonymous with the Femme Fatale archetype.

The role of mystery in communication lies in its ability to captivate the audience's curiosity and attention. You can create a spooky atmosphere that draws people in by sharing just enough information to intrigue while holding back enough to leave them wanting more. However, creating mystery isn't about being dishonest or secretive; it's about selective sharing. It's about revealing your thoughts, feelings, and experiences at your own pace and comfort level, thus maintaining your autonomy and mystique.

Subtlety, on the other hand, is a sophisticated art of implication. It's about expressing your thoughts and feelings in nuanced ways that invite interpretation rather than stating them explicitly. Subtle communication can involve understated gestures, indirect speech, or implied meanings. It requires high emotional intelligence and discernment, both in expressing and interpreting subtle cues.

The use of mystery and subtlety in communication can serve several purposes:

- It can make your interactions more engaging and dynamic. When people sense there's more to discover about you, they're more likely to be drawn to you.
- It can give you greater control over your narrative. You decide what to reveal, when, and to whom, thus protecting your privacy and maintaining your independence.
- It may give your identity more nuance and complexity, making you more captivating and memorable.

However, it's crucial to strike a balance. Too much mystery can come across as aloof or disinterested while overdoing subtlety can lead to miscommunication or confusion. The key lies in adjusting your approach according to the situation and the person you're communicating with.

In embodying the Femme Fatale, the roles of mystery and subtlety can't be understated. These elements contribute significantly to her captivating charm and charisma. By mastering these skills, you can enhance your communication, intrigue your audience, and assert your autonomy, embodying the spirit of the Femme Fatale - a woman who is confident, captivating, and unapologetically mysterious.

CHAPTER 6

THE POWER OF EMOTIONAL INTELLIGENCE

Embracing the power and charisma of the Femme Fatale archetype involves understanding and effectively managing your own emotions. It is about mastering emotional intelligence - a key element in the journey toward personal development and empowerment.

The capacity to identify, comprehend, and control our own emotions and other people's emotions is called emotional intelligence. Emotions form the underpinning of our reactions to life's challenges and opportunities. Understanding our dynamic landscape gives us deeper insights into ourselves, guiding our actions and interpersonal relationships and influencing our mental health.

The first step to understanding and managing your emotions is self-awareness. This involves acknowledging your feelings without judgment, understanding what triggers them, and recognizing their impact on your thoughts and behaviors. It's about listening to your emotions, which can provide valuable information about your needs and desires.

Mindfulness is a valuable practice to enhance self-awareness. By focusing on the present moment, you can observe your emotions as they arise without getting swept away by them. Mindfulness allows you to distance yourself from your feelings, viewing them as transient rather than defining characteristics.

As a robust technique for emotional self-awareness, journaling may also be used. By writing about your sentiments, you can obtain fresh insights and a deeper understanding. It offers a safe space to express your emotions freely, enhancing your knowledge.

Once you've understood your emotions, the next step is learning to manage them effectively. Emotional regulation involves managing and responding to your feelings in a socially acceptable way and beneficial to your well-being.

One effective strategy for emotional regulation is cognitive reappraisal. This involves reframing your perspective on a situation to alter its emotional impact. For example, viewing a failure as a learning opportunity rather than a personal flaw can alleviate negative emotions and foster resilience.

Another strategy is emotion-focused coping, which involves finding ways to soothe yourself when upset. This might be achieved by using relaxing methods like meditation or deep breathing, partaking in activities you enjoy, or asking for help from loved ones.

Constructively expressing your emotions is also crucial. Bottling up your feelings can lead to increased stress and emotional overwhelm. Instead, find healthy outlets for expression, such as talking to a trusted friend, engaging in creative activities, or seeking professional help.

Managing your emotions also involves taking care of your physical health. Regular exercise, a balanced diet, sufficient sleep, and avoiding harmful substances can significantly impact your emotional well-being. Physical and emotional health are deeply interconnected; neglecting one can adversely affect the other.

Emotional intelligence also extends to recognizing and understanding the emotions of others, known as empathy. Being attuned to others' feelings allows you to interact with them more effectively and build stronger, more meaningful relationships.

Understanding and managing your emotions isn't about suppressing or eliminating them. All emotions, even the uncomfortable ones, are valid and provide valuable information. It's about learning to navigate your emotional landscape with understanding and acceptance, using your emotions as a guide rather than letting them control you.

By mastering emotional intelligence, you can enhance your personal and interpersonal effectiveness, improve your mental well-being, and become more resilient. It allows you to handle life's ups and downs with grace and poise, just like the Femme Fatale - a woman who is confident, charismatic, emotionally savvy, and resilient. It is a journey of self-discovery and growth, empowering you to lead a more authentic, fulfilling, and emotionally balanced life.

Reading and responding to others' emotions

The ability to accurately read and respond to others' emotions, often termed empathy, is a significant aspect of emotional intelligence and an inherent trait of the Femme Fatale archetype. It enhances interpersonal relationships, fosters mutual understanding, and allows for effective communication, playing a crucial role in personal and professional life.

Reading emotions requires empathy, which is the capacity to comprehend and experience other people's feelings. It involves seeing the world from someone else's perspective and connecting with their emotional experience. This connection fosters a sense of trust and understanding, creating more profound, more meaningful relationships.

Emotional cues can often be found in non-verbal signals. Observing a person's facial expressions, body language, and tone of voice can provide insights into their emotional state. For instance, crossed arms might indicate defensiveness, while a warm tone might suggest friendliness or comfort.

Active listening is another essential tool for reading emotions. This involves paying full attention to the speaker, reflecting on what they've said to confirm understanding, and withholding judgment or advice unless it's sought. By truly listening, you can pick up on the feelings and needs underlying their words, fostering understanding and connection.

Once you've read another person's emotions, the next step is responding appropriately. This response should respect and consider the other person's feelings and perspective. It's about validating their emotions - acknowledging them without trying to change, dismiss, or judge them. Validation communicates that you see and accept their feelings, even if you don't necessarily agree with their perspective.

Effective responses often involve expressing empathy and offering support. This could be as simple as saying, "That sounds hard," or "I'm here for you." It's not about solving their problems but offering emotional support and understanding.

In certain situations, managing others' emotions might be appropriate. This could involve calming someone upset, encouraging someone who's down, or gently confronting someone who's misbehaving. However, it's essential to approach this with respect and consideration for the other person's autonomy.

Responding to others' emotions also involves managing your own emotions. Remaining calm and composed, especially when faced with intense emotions, allows you to respond effectively. This often requires self-awareness and self-regulation - understanding and managing your emotional reactions appropriately.

Cultivating the ability to read and respond to others' emotions takes practice and patience. It involves developing empathy and observation skills and practicing active listening and effective communication. However, the effort is well worth it. You can increase your emotional intelligence and grow more robust, fulfilling relationships, navigate social situations gracefully, and respond to life's challenges with understanding and resilience - much like the Femme Fatale, a woman of charisma, emotional depth, and irresistible allure.

Navigating complex social dynamics

Navigating complex social dynamics is a vital skill in the quest to embody the Femme Fatale archetype. This process involves understanding and maneuvering intricate interactions, managing interpersonal relationships, and utilizing social influence and power dynamics to your advantage. In essence, this journey is about understanding the art of social intelligence.

Social intelligence, the ability to understand and efficiently navigate and negotiate complicated social contexts, is critical to social survival and success. It involves understanding and interpreting social cues, managing and regulating emotions within social interactions, and adjusting behaviors according to different social situations.

Successful navigation through social dynamics is founded on understanding your colonial style and how it interacts with others. Some people are more assertive, others more cooperative. Some are naturally more outgoing and friendly, others more reserved and introverted. Knowing your social style, strengths, and weaknesses can guide you in engaging with others in ways that play to your strengths.

Understanding the social styles and motivations of others is equally important. Please consider their communication styles, behavioral patterns, and emotional responses. This understanding can help you predict their reactions, tailor your approach, and build more effective and harmonious relationships.

Effective communication is another critical element of navigating social dynamics. This involves speaking clearly and assertively, listening attentively, and responding empathetically. It's about expressing your thoughts and feelings respectfully and appropriately while also being receptive to the thoughts and feelings of others.

Managing conflict is also a crucial aspect of navigating social dynamics. Conflict is inevitable in social interactions but doesn't have to be destructive. It can be an opportunity for growth and improved understanding. The key is managing conflict constructively - expressing your viewpoints assertively but respectfully, understanding and acknowledging the other person's perspective, and seeking a satisfactory solution for both parties.

Building strong social networks is another essential element. These networks provide support, companionship, and opportunities for collaboration. They also offer a sense of belonging and purpose, enhancing overall well-being. Building a solid social network involves being reliable, showing interest in others, and offering help and support when needed.

Understanding power dynamics is also essential in navigating social situations. Power dynamics are present in every social interaction and can significantly influence outcomes. Awareness of these dynamics and knowing how to assert your power and influence when needed can enhance your social effectiveness.

Negotiating is another critical skill in managing complex social dynamics. It involves finding a solution that satisfies both parties in a conflict or a deal, balancing between asserting your needs and understanding and accommodating the needs of others.

Another essential facet is the ability to read the room or the social atmosphere in a group setting. This includes understanding group norms, roles, and dynamics and adjusting your behavior accordingly.

Navigating complex social dynamics is not about manipulating others or being inauthentic. It's about understanding social interactions at a deeper level and engaging in them effectively and ethically. It's about fostering meaningful relationships, contributing positively to social situations, and maintaining integrity and authenticity.

The Femme Fatale, with her irresistible charm and charisma, is a master of social dynamics. By developing your social intelligence, you can navigate complex social situations with grace and confidence, build fulfilling relationships, and positively impact your social environment.

CHAPTER 7

THE ART OF SEDUCTION

When we mention the term "seduction," it often conjures images of physical allure, romantic conquests, and sexual attraction. However, in the context of embodying the Femme Fatale archetype, seduction extends far beyond the physical aspect. It's about captivating the minds and hearts of others, stirring emotions, and inspiring action. It's about personal charisma, the power of influence, and the art of persuasion.

To redefine seduction, we first must understand that it is an integral part of human interaction. Seduction isn't merely about romantic or sexual attraction but the power to attract, engage, and influence. In essence, seduction is a form of communication, an interactive process between the seducer and the seduced.

At its core, seduction involves arousing interest and curiosity, creating a sense of intrigue and desire. This isn't limited to physical allure; it can also be achieved through intellectual stimulation, emotional resonance, and shared values or interests.

Intellectual seduction involves engaging the mind. This can be achieved through stimulating conversations, academic challenges, or shared passions. It's about showing your depth of understanding, wit, and insights. It's about showcasing your intelligence and creativity, making people think and wonder, and leaving them craving more.

Emotional seduction, on the other hand, involves connecting on a deeper emotional level. This involves understanding and resonating with the emotions of others, sharing meaningful experiences, and expressing genuine empathy and understanding. It's about creating emotional bonds, making people feel valued and understood, and stirring powerful emotions.

Seduction can also be achieved through shared values or interests. This involves finding common ground, connecting over shared passions or goals, and building a sense of camaraderie and mutual understanding. It's about showing that you value the same things, that you're part of the same tribe, and that you're on the same journey.

Moreover, effective seduction involves a sense of mystery and suspense. This consists in revealing enough to pique interest but not so much as to eliminate intrigue. It's about leaving them wanting more, guessing your next move, and looking forward to your subsequent encounter.

Seduction also involves a balance between attraction and challenge. While it's essential to show interest and make the other person feel desired, it's equally important to maintain a certain level of autonomy and self-worth. This involves asserting your boundaries, defending your interests and passions, and showing that you're a person of value worth pursuing.

Redefining seduction in this way elevates it from a shallow pursuit of physical attraction to a nuanced art of influence and engagement. It transforms seduction from a game of conquest to a dance of connection, intrigue, and mutual enrichment.

The Femme Fatale, with her captivating charm and charismatic presence, embodies this redefined concept of seduction. She understands that seduction is not about manipulation or deception but about authentic connection, mutual respect, and the art of influence. She uses seduction not to conquer or control but to captivate, inspire, and create meaningful connections.

By redefining seduction, you, too, can learn to wield its power effectively and ethically. You can captivate minds, stir emotions, and inspire action, not just through your physical presence but through your intellect, your feelings, and your authentic self. You can become a true Femme Fatale, a woman of irresistible allure and powerful influence.

Building emotional and intellectual connections

In the Femme Fatale archetype context, building emotional and intellectual connections is a multifaceted endeavor that revolves around self-understanding, empathic listening, mutual respect, shared interests, and meaningful conversation. It's about attracting others not just with physical allure but with your intellect, your emotions, and your authentic self.

Self-Understanding and Emotional Intelligence

The foundation of building emotional and intellectual connections is self-understanding and emotional intelligence. This involves understanding your emotions, motivations, strengths, and weaknesses and managing your emotions effectively.

Self-understanding begins with introspection. Reflect on your experiences, thoughts, and feelings. Understand what makes you happy, what makes you upset, and what motivates you. This understanding will guide your interactions with others, helping you communicate your feelings and needs more effectively.

Understanding and controlling your emotions are essential components of emotional intelligence, understanding and responding to the feelings of others. It requires empathy, the ability to share and understand the feelings of others, which is crucial in building emotional connections.

Empathic Listening

Empathic listening involves listening with the intent to understand rather than to respond. It's about putting you in the other person's shoes, understanding their perspective, and validating their feelings and experiences.

When you listen empathically, you hear the words the other person is saying and pick up on their underlying feelings, needs, and concerns. This fosters understanding and trust, making the other person feel valued and understood and building a deeper emotional connection.

Mutual Respect

Mutual regard is essential to creating emotional and intellectual connections. This involves respecting the other person's feelings, thoughts, and experiences and treating them with kindness and consideration.

When you show respect, you communicate that you value the other person and their perspective. This fosters a sense of safety and trust, creating a solid foundation for a deeper connection.

Shared Interests

Shared interests provide a common ground for building intellectual connections. They provide a topic for conversation, a shared experience, and a mutual goal or passion.

Having shared interests makes conversation flow more efficiently, as you can discuss something you both enjoy. It also allows you to share experiences, learn from each other, and grow together, strengthening your intellectual bond.

Meaningful Conversation

Meaningful conversation involves:

- Discussing essential topics with both parties.
- Expressing thoughts and feelings openly and honestly.
- Seeking to understand and learn from each other.

It's about sharing ideas, challenging each other's perspectives, and building mutual understanding and respect.

Meaningful conversation not only stimulates the mind but also stirs emotions. It makes you think, feel, and reflect, deepening your emotional and intellectual bond.

Building emotional and intellectual connections is a dynamic, ongoing process. It requires patience, understanding, and genuine interest in the other person. It's not about impressing or dominating but connecting, understanding, and growing together.

The Femme Fatale, with her irresistible charm and depth of character, understands the power of emotional and intellectual connections. She doesn't just attract others with her physical allure but also captivates them with her intellect, emotions, and authentic self. By building deep, meaningful connections, she creates a powerful attraction beyond the physical, drawing others into her world and leaving an indelible impact.

The ethical side of seduction

As with any interaction that wields influence over others, seduction requires a solid ethical foundation. It is vital to understand that the power of seduction must be exercised with respect, authenticity, and genuine consideration for the well-being of all parties involved. This is not about manipulation or deception but fostering real connections and mutual understanding.

Respect and Consent

At the core of ethical seduction is respect and consent. Respect involves:

- Acknowledging the other person's autonomy and personal boundaries.
- Appreciating their unique perspectives.
- Treating them with dignity and consideration.

Conversely, consent is about ensuring that your actions and advances are welcomed and reciprocated.

Both respect and consent are crucial in maintaining the integrity of your interactions. They ensure that your actions are guided by a regard for the other person's comfort, preferences, and well-being. Ethical seduction is not about coercion or manipulation but creating a mutually satisfying connection based on trust and understanding.

Authenticity

Authenticity is another vital aspect of ethical seduction. It's about being genuine in your intentions, honest in your communication, and true to your values and identity.

This doesn't mean revealing everything about you simultaneously – a degree of mystery can be enticing. However, what you do tell should be truthful and genuine. Authenticity fosters trust and deeper connections and helps ensure that any relationship developed is based on a fundamental understanding and appreciation of each other.

Empathy and Understanding

Understanding and experiencing another person's emotions are required for empathy. It's about stepping into their shoes, seeing the world from their perspective, and responding with kindness and consideration.

Empathy allows you to connect on a deeper emotional level in the context of seduction. It helps you to understand the other person's needs, desires, and concerns and to respond in a way that makes them feel valued and understood.

Balance and Mutuality

Ethical seduction also involves maintaining a balance of power and ensuring mutuality. This means avoiding situations where one party is overly dominant or where the connection is primarily one-sided.

A balanced, mutual connection is more satisfying and sustainable. It allows both parties to contribute to and benefit from the relationship, fostering a sense of equality and shared enjoyment.

Well-being Well-being and Positive Impact

Finally, ethical seduction should contribute to the well-being of all parties involved and have a positive impact. This consists of considering your actions' potential consequences and striving to ensure that your interactions lead to positive outcomes.

The goal of seduction should not be to take advantage of others but to enrich your experiences and relationships. It's about creating connections that bring joy, growth, and positive transformation.

The ethical side of seduction is about ensuring that your actions are guided by respect, authenticity, empathy, balance, and genuine concern for all parties' well-being. It's about using the power of seduction responsibly to create authentic connections, enrich relationships, and make a positive impact.

The Femme Fatale, with her irresistible allure and powerful influence, understands and embodies this ethical approach to seduction. She wields her power with grace and consideration, captivating the minds and hearts of others, not through manipulation or deception but through genuine connection, mutual respect, and the art of ethical influence. By embodying this honest approach, you, too, can wield the power of seduction effectively and responsibly, creating meaningful connections and leaving a positive and lasting impact.

CHAPTER 8

FEMME FATALE IN RELATIONSHIPS

Boundaries, in the context of personal interactions and relationships, are fundamental to maintaining healthy dynamics and ensuring mutual respect. They serve as guidelines for ourselves and others about what we find acceptable, comfortable, and respectful. Setting and respecting boundaries is essential for self-preservation and forms the cornerstone of ethical interactions.

Understanding Boundaries

Boundaries can be considered invisible lines that define the limits of our personal space, comfort, and well-being. Depending on the context, they can be physical, emotional, mental, or even digital. Physical boundaries, for instance, might concern personal space or touch, while emotional boundaries might involve privacy, feelings, and unique experiences.

Understanding your boundaries involves self-reflection and introspection. It requires you to identify what makes you feel comfortable, safe, unsafe, respected, or disrespected. It requires you to understand your needs, values, and limitations and communicate them to others.

Setting Boundaries

Setting boundaries is a proactive process that involves clearly defining and communicating your limits to others. It's about expressing your needs and expectations clearly, directly, and respectfully.

To set effective boundaries, you need to understand and assert your self-worth. You have the right to define your limits and to expect others to respect them. You also have the responsibility to respect the boundaries of others and to respond to their needs and concerns with understanding and consideration.

Respecting Boundaries

Respecting boundaries involves understanding and honoring the limits set by others. It's about showing empathy, consideration, and respect for their comfort, safety, and well-being.

Respecting boundaries also involves being attentive and responsive. It requires you to listen actively, observe non-verbal cues, and respond in a considerate and respectful manner. If you're unsure about someone's boundaries, asking and respecting their response is essential.

Navigating Boundary Challenges

Despite our best efforts, boundary challenges can arise. These can be situations where our boundaries are not respected, where we struggle to respect the boundaries of others, or where our borders conflict with those of others.

Navigating these challenges requires communication, negotiation, and sometimes compromise. It involves expressing your concerns clearly and respectfully, seeking to understand the other person's perspective, Considering the other person's viewpoint, and cooperating to develop a workable solution are necessary.

The Power of Boundaries

Boundaries are not just about preventing harm or discomfort. They also can foster mutual respect, deepen connections, and enrich interactions.

You feel valued, understood, and safe when your boundaries are respected. You can express yourself authentically, engage fully, and contribute meaningfully. When you appreciate the boundaries of others, you demonstrate empathy, consideration, and respect, fostering trust and deepening your connection.

Setting and respecting boundaries is fundamental to ethical, respectful interactions. The Femme Fatale, with her captivating allure and influential power, understands the importance of boundaries. She sets and respects boundaries, ensuring her interactions are based on mutual respect and understanding. This safeguards her well-being, fosters trust, deepens connections, and enriches her relationships. By experience, setting, and respecting boundaries, you, too, can create meaningful, respectful interactions and cultivate a powerful and authentic presence.

Navigating romance and passion with poise

Maintaining composure and navigating the intricate dance with grace and poise can be challenging in the realm of romance and passion. As a modern Femme Fatale, the mastery of maintaining your balance amidst the highs and lows of romantic engagements will set you apart, infusing your relationships with an irresistible allure and depth.

Understanding the Nature of Romance and Passion

Romance and passion, although intoxicating, can often lead us down a path of overwhelming emotions. It's essential to remember that these feelings, while intense, are part and parcel of human interactions. Passion brings joy and excitement, while romance provides connection and intimacy. Understanding these emotions' nature and accepting them as natural parts of the human experience is the first step towards navigating them with poise.

Maintaining Self-Awareness

In the throes of passion or the tenderness of romance, it's easy to lose oneself. Therefore, maintaining self-awareness is crucial.

This means recognizing your emotions, understanding your desires, and being aware of your actions. It's about constantly checking in with yourself, assessing your feelings, and making sure your actions align with your core values. Remember, losing individuality or compromising your values for romance or passion can lead to dissatisfaction and regret.

Effective Communication

Each love relationship must be built on open and honest communication. Expressing your feelings, needs, and expectations clearly and honestly is crucial. Whether it's about expressing affection, addressing concerns, or setting boundaries, effective communication ensures that both parties understand and can fulfill each other's needs while maintaining respect and consideration.

Emotional Intelligence

Navigating romance and passion with poise requires emotional intelligence. This means understanding and managing your emotions, as well as empathizing with the feelings of your partner. Emotional intelligence allows you to respond to situations with maturity and sensitivity, helping you maintain poise even in challenging situations.

Maintaining Balance

Balance is critical in navigating romance and passion. It's about not losing your sense of self amidst the romantic whirlwind and ensuring you're investing time and energy in other important aspects of your life, such as personal growth, friendships, hobbies, and career. Keeping a balanced perspective helps you enjoy the thrill of romance and passion while staying grounded and poised.

Resilience in the Face of Setbacks

Romantic interactions may sometimes go differently than planned. It's essential to face these situations with resilience. This involves accepting reality, learning from the experience, and positively moving forward. Stability allows you to navigate the world of romance and passion with strength and poise, even in the face of setbacks.

Navigating romance and passion with poise requires understanding and acceptance of the nature of these emotions, maintaining self-awareness and balance, communicating effectively, harnessing emotional intelligence, and displaying resilience in the face of setbacks. By mastering these skills, you can embrace the world of romance and passion with the elegance and allure of the Femme Fatale, creating enriching relationships that reflect your depth, charisma, and authentic power.

Ensuring emotional well-being and mutual respect

Ensuring emotional well-being and mutual respect are essential aspects of any relationship, whether romantic or otherwise. As a modern Femme Fatale, it's crucial to prioritize emotional well-being, both for yourself and your partner, and to foster a relationship built on respect, trust, and understanding.

Prioritizing Emotional Well-Being

Emotional well-being involves taking care of your mental and emotional health and supporting your partner's emotional well-being. It's about recognizing and understanding your emotions, practicing self-care, and seeking support when needed. Emotional well-being also involves being attuned to your partner's emotions and offering comfort and support during challenging times.

As a Femme Fatale, you understand the importance of self-awareness and emotional intelligence. You know that taking care of your emotional well-being benefits you and positively impacts your relationships. By prioritizing emotional well-being, you can cultivate a sense of inner strength and resilience, enabling you to navigate emotional challenges with grace and poise.

Cultivating Empathy and Understanding

Empathy is crucial in ensuring mutual respect and emotional well-being inside a union. Putting oneself in your partner's shoes entails understanding their feelings and experiences and responding with kindness and compassion.

Cultivating empathy allows you to form a deeper connection with your partner, showing that you genuinely care about their feelings and experiences. Also, it makes it easier for you to comprehend and respond to their wants and concerns through communication.

Communicating with Respect and Sensitivity

Good communication is necessary in every relationship, but it's essential when it comes to respect and emotional well-being. It involves expressing yourself honestly and assertively while being mindful of your partner's feelings and reactions.

Avoiding blame or criticism and using "I" statements can promote a more positive and constructive communication style. For example, saying, "I feel hurt when..." rather than "You always do this..." helps keep the focus on your feelings and experiences rather than making your partner feel attacked.

Setting and Respecting Boundaries

Boundaries play a significant role in maintaining emotional well-being and mutual respect. Establishing clear boundaries helps define what is acceptable and comfortable for you and your partner. It allows you to protect your emotional well-being and ensures that your relationship is based on mutual understanding and respect.

Respecting each other's boundaries is equally important. It shows that you value and respect your partner's needs and preferences. If a limit is crossed, it's crucial to communicate about it openly and honestly, seeking understanding and resolution.

Nurturing Trust and Security

Each healthy relationship is built on trust. Nurturing trust involves being reliable, consistent, and honest in your actions and words. It also means keeping your promises and being accountable for your efforts.

Creating a sense of emotional security in the relationship allows both partners to feel safe and supported. Emotional security allows for vulnerability and emotional intimacy, as both partners can trust that their feelings and experiences will be respected and cared for.

Ensuring emotional well-being and mutual respect in a relationship requires prioritizing emotional health, cultivating empathy and understanding, communicating with care and sensitivity, setting and respecting boundaries, and nurturing trust and security. As a modern Femme Fatale, embodying these principles will help you build relationships with depth, emotional connection, and authentic power.

CHAPTER 9

FEMME FATALES AND PROFESSIONAL SUCCESS

The Femme Fatale archetype is not limited to romance or personal relationships. It can also be an influential asset in the professional world, offering a unique set of traits and skills that can drive career growth and success. Embodying the Femme Fatale traits in the workplace can help you stand out, build strong professional relationships, and navigate complex career dynamics with confidence and allure.

Confidence and Self-Assurance

Confidence is a key trait of the Femme Fatale and is equally crucial in the professional arena. Confidence exudes a sense of self-assurance and belief in one's abilities, which can inspire trust and respect from colleagues, superiors, and clients.

Embracing your inner Femme Fatale means having the self-assurance to take on challenges, speak up, and assert your ideas and opinions.

Charisma and Networking Skills

The Femme Fatale is known for her charismatic presence and magnetic allure, which can be invaluable in networking and building professional relationships. As people are more apt to notice and value your abilities and accomplishments, this may result in greater possibilities for growth and success in your profession. Making a significant and lasting impression can open doors to new opportunities and partnerships. A key element of job growth is networking.

With your Femme Fatale traits, you can approach networking with confidence and charm. You can engage in meaningful conversations, establish rapport with others, and leave a lasting positive impression. By using these talents, you may broaden your professional network, learn insightful things, and find new job possibilities.

Emotional Intelligence and Communication

The Femme Fatale is emotionally intelligent and attuned to her feelings and those of others. In the workplace, emotional intelligence is valuable for effective communication and building strong professional relationships.

Emotional intelligence allows you to navigate office dynamics with poise, respond empathetically to colleagues' needs and concerns, and address conflicts with diplomacy. This can lead to smoother interactions and better teamwork, ultimately contributing to a more positive and productive work environment.

Negotiation and Persuasion

Persuasion is a skill the Femme Fatale wields to significant effect, and it is equally powerful in the business world. Effective persuasion can help you negotiate better deals, influence decision-making, and advocate for your ideas and proposals.

By honing your persuasion skills, you can present your viewpoints with compelling arguments, anticipate and address counterarguments, and convince others of the value of your contributions. This can increase recognition for your expertise and accomplishments, paving the way for career advancement.

Adaptability and Resilience

The Femme Fatale is no stranger to challenges and setbacks but maintains her allure and strength in the face of adversity. In the professional realm, adaptability and resilience are essential for career growth.

You may successfully traverse the corporate world's dynamic nature by being able to adjust to changing circumstances, learn from mistakes, and overcome setbacks. Embracing your Femme Fatale traits means approaching challenges with determination and grace, turning obstacles into opportunities for growth and development.

Leveraging Femme Fatale traits for career growth involves:

- Embracing confidence and self-assurance.
- Harnessing charisma and networking skills.
- Applying emotional intelligence and effective communication.
- Honing negotiation and persuasion abilities.
- Cultivating adaptability and resilience.

By embodying these traits, you can stand out professionally, build strong relationships, and propel your career to new heights with allure and poise.

Balancing ambition with personal life

Balancing ambition with personal life is a common challenge many individuals face, especially those striving for career success. As a modern Femme Fatale, achieving this balance requires mastering the art of prioritization, setting boundaries, practicing self-care, and maintaining a sense of authenticity and fulfillment in both aspects of life.

Clarifying Your Priorities

Balancing ambition with personal life starts with clarifying your priorities. Take the time to reflect on what truly matters to you. What are your career goals and aspirations? What are your personal goals and values? Understanding what is most important to you will help guide your decision-making and time allocation.

That your priorities may shift over time, and that's perfectly normal. It's essential to regularly reassess and realign your goals and values to ensure that you are consistently moving towards a fulfilling and balanced life.

Setting Boundaries

Setting boundaries is crucial for maintaining a balance between ambition and personal life. This involves defining clear limits for work and personal time and ensuring that one aspect does not infringe on the other.

Have reasonable expectations regarding your availability with your employer and coworkers outside of business hours. Learn to say no to excessive work demands when it interferes with your commitments. Similarly, establish boundaries in your personal life to protect your time and energy for self-care and family.

Practicing Effective Time Management

Time management is a vital skill for achieving a balance between ambition and personal life. Organize your schedule to allocate time for work, personal pursuits, and leisure activities. Use to-do lists, calendars, and productivity apps to stay organized and on track.

Set priorities for your work and pay attention to the most crucial ones first. This will enable you to efficiently complete your career objectives while freeing up more time for your personal life. Avoid overcommitting yourself, and learn to delegate tasks when appropriate to lighten your workload.

Embracing Self-Care

Self-care is essential for maintaining well-being and avoiding burnout. Making self-care a priority is necessary to succeed in your personal and professional life as a contemporary Femme Fatale.

Discover ways to relax and re-energize yourself, such as via exercise, meditation, hobbies, or spending time with loved ones.

Make time to unwind; a well-rested mind is more creative and productive.

Emphasizing Quality over Quantity

Balance doesn't necessarily mean spending equal time on career and personal pursuits. Instead, focus on the quality of the time you invest in each aspect of your life.

When you are at work, be fully present and productive. Avoid distractions and prioritize tasks that align with your career goals. Similarly, when you are with family and friends, please give them your undivided attention and create meaningful connections.

Maintaining Authenticity and Fulfillment

Last but not least, ensuring that your personal and professional lives are in harmony with your true selves and fulfill you is critical. Pursuing a career that resonates with your passions and values will make your professional journey more rewarding and meaningful.

Similarly, ensure that your personal life is enriched with activities and relationships that bring joy and satisfaction. Nurture your passions, hobbies, and personal growth to maintain a sense of fulfillment outside of work.

Dealing with professional challenges and setbacks

Challenges and setbacks are unavoidable when pursuing achievement. As a modern Femme Fatale, you can navigate these obstacles gracefully and resiliently. When faced with professional challenges, it's crucial to approach them with a positive mindset and a problem-solving attitude. Instead of viewing setbacks as failures, see them as opportunities for growth and learning. Embrace challenges as stepping stones that will lead you to more significant achievements.

When confronted with setbacks, take the time to reflect on the situation and identify any lessons or insights that can be gained from the experience. Use setbacks to reassess your strategies and make necessary adjustments to your approach. Remember that setbacks are a natural part of the journey to success and do not define your worth or capabilities.

Seek support from mentors, colleagues, or friends who can offer guidance and encouragement during challenging times. A solid support system might provide you with new views and insights that could help you tackle challenges more successfully.

In the face of difficulty, maintain your grit and persistence. Adopting a "never give up" attitude will propel you forward, even during the most challenging moments. Embrace failures as stepping stones towards success, and let them fuel your determination to achieve your goals.

Additionally, focus on maintaining a healthy work-life balance. Avoid allowing setbacks to consume your personal life. Engaging in activities you enjoy outside work can help you recharge and regain perspective. Taking care of your well-being is essential for building the strength to tackle professional challenges.

Dealing with professional challenges and setbacks as a modern Femme Fatale involves:

- Embracing challenges as opportunities for growth.
- Reflecting on the lessons learned.
- Seeking support from your network.
- Staying resilient.

- Maintaining a healthy work-life balance.

By navigating challenges with grace and perseverance, you can emerge more robust and empowered, ready to conquer the next chapter of your career journey.

CHAPTER 10

CHALLENGING STEREOTYPES AND MISCONCEPTIONS

The Femme Fatale archetype has been a subject of fascination and intrigue for centuries, often portrayed as a dangerous and manipulative woman who uses her charm to seduce and harm others. However, it is essential to challenge these societal prejudices and misconceptions surrounding Femme Fatales and recognize this archetype's empowering and multifaceted nature.

One of the fundamental misconceptions about Femme Fatales is that they are solely focused on manipulating others for personal gain. Femme Fatales can be strong, independent, and intelligent women who use their allure and charisma to navigate a male-dominated world and assert their agency.

Addressing these prejudices involves understanding the historical context of the Femme Fatale archetype. In many traditional narratives, Femme Fatales were depicted as femme fatale archetypes, and by exploring their complexities, we can break free from limiting stereotypes and celebrate the diversity and strength of women's characters.

Moreover, it is crucial to recognize that the Femme Fatale archetype should not be limited to cisgender women. Femme Fatales can be individuals of any gender with alluring and powerful qualities. Acknowledging this can create a more inclusive and diverse understanding of the Femme Fatale archetype.

Another misconception is that Femme Fatales are solely driven by their physical appearance. In reality, the power of Femme Fatales lies in their confidence, intelligence, and ability to command attention with their presence and charisma.

To address these prejudices, we must celebrate women and individuals who embody the Femme Fatale archetype for their intelligence, independence, and assertiveness rather than reducing them to superficial and manipulative characters.

Furthermore, it is crucial to recognize that women should not be confined to societal expectations or stereotypes. Embracing the Femme Fatale archetype means embracing the freedom to express oneself authentically, irrespective of societal norms.

Promoting diverse and empowering representations of Femme Fatales in media and literature can also help challenge these prejudices. By showcasing well-rounded and complex characters, we can shift the narrative around the Femme Fatale archetype and present a more nuanced perspective.

Lastly, engaging in open conversations and dialogues about the Femme Fatale archetype can help dispel myths and challenge societal prejudices. We can encourage a more upbeat and welcoming understanding by discussing the empowering aspects of this archetype and its potential for character growth and transformation.

Turning criticism into strength

Criticism is an inevitable part of life, and as a modern Femme Fatale, you can transform it into a source of strength and growth.

Rather than letting criticism bring you down, use it as an opportunity to learn, evolve, and become even more powerful.

One way to turn criticism into strength is by adopting a growth mindset. Embrace the idea that challenges and feedback are opportunities for improvement and self-development. Instead of viewing criticism as a personal attack, see it as valuable information that can help you identify areas for growth.

Next, take a moment to reflect on the criticism objectively. Separate the emotions from the feedback and try to see it from an outsider's perspective. Look for any grains of truth in the complaint, even if it is difficult to accept. Acknowledging your weaknesses can be the first step towards turning them into strengths.

Use criticism as a motivation to push yourself further. Channel the negative energy into a determination to prove the critics wrong. Let their words fuel your drive to excel and show them you are resilient and capable of overcoming challenges.

Seek feedback and advice from trusted mentors or colleagues who can offer constructive criticism. They can provide insights and guidance on effectively addressing areas of improvement. Having a support system can make it easier to navigate through criticism and turn it into a positive force in your life.

Keep in mind that mistakes are typical and that nobody is flawless. Embrace failure as a stepping stone toward success. Learn from your errors, make the necessary adjustments, and keep moving forward with even greater determination.

Turning criticism into strength also involves developing a strong sense of self-belief and self-worth. Remind yourself of your successes, abilities, and the value you offer. Develop your confidence and use it as a shield against the world's negativity.

Finally, don't be afraid to stand up for yourself when faced with unfair or unfounded criticism. Be assertive and vocal in expressing your thoughts and defending your actions. Show that you are confident in your abilities and willing to learn and grow, but also demand respect and fair treatment.

Turning criticism into strength involves adopting a growth mindset, reflecting on feedback objectively, seeking guidance from mentors, using criticism as motivation, embracing failure, developing self-belief, and standing up for yourself. As a modern Femme Fatale, you can transform criticism into a driving force that propels you toward success and empowers you to become the best version of yourself.

Advocating for respect and understanding

As a modern Femme Fatale, you can advocate for respect and understanding in your personal and professional relationships. Embodying the traits of the Femme Fatale archetype, you can inspire positive change and promote a culture of empathy, inclusivity, and mutual respect.

Advocating for respect and understanding starts with leading by example. Treat others with kindness, empathy, and respect, regardless of their background, beliefs, or opinions. Show that you value diversity and actively listen to different perspectives without judgment.

In the workplace, foster a culture of respect by encouraging free dialogue and creating a secure environment for colleagues to express their ideas and concerns. Encourage collaboration and teamwork, recognizing that diverse perspectives can lead to innovative solutions.

Address any instances of discrimination or disrespect that you witness or experience. Use your voice and influence to stand up for yourself and others. Encourage those around you to do the same, establishing a welcoming atmosphere where everyone feels heard and respected.

Educate others about the importance of respect and understanding. Organize workshops or discussions to raise awareness of unconscious biases and stereotypes and their impact on relationships and productivity. Encourage ongoing learning and self-reflection to promote personal growth and increase awareness of diversity's value.

Practice active listening and empathy in your interactions. Seek to understand others' experiences and perspectives, even if they differ from your own. This will facilitate the development of an understanding-based environment and lessen disputes or misunderstandings.

Promote laws and procedures that encourage diversity and inclusion in your workplace or community. Support initiatives to create a more equitable, safe, and courteous atmosphere for everyone regardless of their identity or heritage.

Be a humble leader who is open to receiving advice from others. Realize that no one has all the answers and that we can all learn from others' experiences and points of view. Accept criticism as a chance for development and progress.

Celebrate and uplift the voices of marginalized individuals and communities. Use your platform and influence to amplify their stories and experiences. Encourage others to do the same and promote a more inclusive and equitable society.

As a modern Femme Fatale, you can advocate for respect and understanding. Embodying the traits of the Femme Fatale archetype, you can inspire positive change in your personal and professional relationships. By leading with empathy, promoting diversity and inclusion, standing up against discrimination, and actively listening to With the help of others, you may establish a climate of tolerance and respect that is advantageous to all parties involved and promotes harmony and togetherness.

CHAPTER 11

THE FEMME FATALE LIFESTYLE

Embracing the Femme Fatale archetype goes beyond adopting a persona; it is about designing a life that reflects your inner power, allure, and authenticity. As a modern Femme Fatale, you can create a life that aligns with your passions, values, and aspirations. By harnessing the traits of the Femme Fatale, you can craft a life filled with purpose, confidence, and fulfillment.

Embracing Your Inner Femme Fatale

Designing your life as a Femme Fatale begins with embracing your inner power and allure. Recognize and celebrate your unique qualities, strengths, and talents. Embrace your confidence, intelligence, and charisma. Embody the charm and magnetism that sets you apart from the crowd.

Avoid the temptation to conform to societal norms or expectations. Instead, follow your path and make decisions that resonate with your true self. Embracing your inner Femme Fatale is about being authentic and unapologetically yourself.

Identifying Your Passions and Purpose

To design a fulfilling life, identify your passions and purpose. Take the time to explore what truly brings you joy and fulfillment. What activities or pursuits make you feel alive and engaged? What causes or issues ignite your passion?

Once you've identified your passions and purpose, align your life choices and actions accordingly. Pursue opportunities and careers that allow you to express your desires and make a positive impact. Let your goal

Setting Bold Goals and Ambitions

As a Femme Fatale, you must dream big and set ambitious goals. Define what success means to you and set bold aspirations. Allow your dreams to be the driving force behind your actions and choices.

Your objectives should be broken down into doable steps create a plan to achieve them. In the face of difficulties, maintain your dedication and fortitude. Remember that setbacks are part of the journey, and embracing your inner Femme Fatale means persevering with grace and determination.

Cultivating Resilience and Confidence

In designing your life as a Femme Fatale, resilience and confidence are essential traits to cultivate. Acquire the capacity to overcome setbacks and disappointments. Make the most of difficulties to gain knowledge and get stronger.

Build your confidence by acknowledging your achievements and celebrating your successes. Avoid self-doubt and negative self-talk. Instead, focus on your capabilities and remind yourself of your power as a modern Femme Fatale.

Creating a Supportive Network

Embrace a community of like-minded people who will support you and inspire you. Create connections with others who share your interests and principles. Seek mentors and role models who will inspire you to accomplish your goals.

A supportive network can provide encouragement, guidance, and valuable insights. At trying times, it may be a source of courage and inspiration. As a Femme Fatale, your network can be instrumental in helping you design a life that aligns with your vision and purpose.

Embracing Work-Life Integration

As you design your life as a Femme Fatale, aim for work-life integration rather than striving for a strict work-life balance. Integrate your passions, purpose, and ambitions into all aspects of your life, including your career, relationships, and personal pursuits.

Avoid compartmentalizing your life and, instead, seek ways to align your work with your passions and values. Find opportunities to infuse your personal life with the sense of allure and magnetism that defines the Femme Fatale archetype.

Prioritizing Self-Care and Well-Being

Designing a fulfilling life as a Femme Fatale requires caring for your well-being. Prioritize self-care and plan activities that nourish your mind, body, and soul. Engage in regular exercise, practice mindfulness, and indulge in activities that bring you joy.

Self-care is not a luxury but a necessity for maintaining balance and resilience. As a modern Femme Fatale, you must nurture your inner strength and allure by caring for yourself with grace and attention.

Celebrating Your Journey

Throughout your journey of designing your life as a Femme Fatale, remember to celebrate every step of the way. Acknowledge your progress and achievements, no matter how small they may seem. Celebrate the person you are becoming and the positive impact you are making.

Celebrate the lessons learned from challenges and the growth that came from setbacks. Embrace your journey as a modern Femme Fatale with grace and gratitude, knowing it is a continuous process of self-discovery and empowerment.

Designing your life as a Femme Fatale involves:

- Embracing your inner power.
- Identifying your passions and purpose.
- Setting bold goals.
- Cultivating resilience and confidence.
- Creating a supportive network.
- Embracing work-life integration.
- Prioritizing self-care.
- Celebrating your journey.

As a modern Femme Fatale, you have the agency to create a life that reflects your true self, embraces your allure, and empowers you to pursue your dreams with grace and determination. By designing a life that aligns with your passions and values, you can embody the essence of the Femme Fatale archetype and lead a fulfilling and purposeful existence.

Daily routines, habits, and rituals of a Femme Fatale

The daily routines, habits, and rituals of a Femme Fatale are essential in maintaining her allure, confidence, and sense of empowerment. By cultivating intentional practices, she sets the stage for success and fulfillment. Here are some key elements that contribute to the daily life of a modern Femme Fatale:

Morning Mindfulness: A Femme Fatale starts her day with mindfulness and intention. She practices gratitude, setting the tone for a positive and empowered mindset. Whether through journaling, meditation, or affirmations, morning mindfulness helps her focus on her goals and priorities for the day ahead.

Physical Well-Being: Maintaining physical health is vital for a Femme Fatale. She engages in regular exercise for fitness and to boost her confidence and energy levels. This could be through dance, yoga, or any form of physical activity that brings her joy and vitality.

Cultivating Elegance: The Femme Fatale pays attention to her appearance and grooming, not out of vanity but as an expression of her self-confidence and allure. She embraces her style, knowing how she presents herself sends a message of empowerment and self-respect to the world.

Intellectual Stimulation: A Femme Fatale is a lifelong learner. She carves time for intellectual stimulation by reading books, engaging in thought-provoking discussions, or pursuing creative endeavors. Academic growth is a crucial aspect of her personal development.

Assertive Communication: The Femme Fatale practices assertive and confident communication in her interactions. She expresses her thoughts and needs clearly and respectfully, setting healthy boundaries and advocating for herself and others.

Networking and Building Relationships: Networking is integral to a Femme Fatale's routine. She actively seeks opportunities to build meaningful connections with others professionally and personally. Creating a supportive network enhances her personal and career growth.

Embracing Solo Time: While she values social interactions, the Femme Fatale embraces solo time for reflection, creativity, and self-renewal. Solitude allows her to reconnect with her inner strength and recharge her allure.

Setting Daily Goals: Each day, the Femme Fatale sets specific and achievable goals aligned with her larger aspirations. She maintains focus and a sense of accomplishment by breaking down her ambitions into daily tasks.

Evening Self-Reflection: As the day winds down, the Femme Fatale self-reflects. She assesses her achievements and areas for improvement, celebrating her successes and learning from any challenges.

Nighttime Rituals: The Femme Fatale practices relaxation rituals to unwind and prepare for restorative sleep before bedtime. This could involve reading, calming skincare routine, or meditation to clear her mind.

Gratitude and Affirmations: Throughout her day, the Femme Fatale practices gratitude and affirmations, reinforcing positive beliefs and attracting abundance and opportunities into her life.

Embracing Spontaneity: While routines are essential, a Femme Fatale also knows the value of spontaneity and adventure. She embraces opportunities for new experiences, which add excitement and growth to her life.

The daily routines, habits, and rituals of a Femme Fatale contribute to her allure, confidence, and sense of empowerment. By cultivating practices that prioritize self-care, self-development, and meaningful connections, she creates a life that aligns with her true self and embodies the essence of the modern Femme Fatale archetype.

Overcoming challenges and obstacles

As a modern Femme Fatale, you are no stranger to challenges and obstacles. You can overcome these hurdles with grace and determination by embracing your inner strength and resilience. Here are some strategies to navigate through challenges and emerge even more empowered:

Embrace a Growth Mindset

- Approach challenges with a growth mindset, recognizing opportunities for learning and growth.
- Instead of seeing setbacks as failures, view them as stepping stones towards success.
- Embrace the belief that you can overcome any obstacles with perseverance and dedication.

Break Challenges into Manageable Steps: When faced with a significant challenge, break it down into smaller, manageable steps. By taking one step at a time, You can retain your sense of progress and avoid feeling overloaded. Celebrate each small victory as they pave the way for conquering the more significant challenge.

Seek Support and Guidance: Don't hesitate to seek support and guidance when facing challenges. Seek advice from mentors, friends, or colleagues who have experienced similar situations. Their insights and encouragement can provide valuable perspectives and strategies for overcoming obstacles.

Reframe Obstacles as Opportunities: By redefining difficulties as chances for development and advancement, you may alter your viewpoint on problems. Embrace the idea that every obstacle presents an opportunity to develop new skills, refine your approach, and deepen your resilience.

Practice Self-Care: During challenging times, prioritize self-care to maintain your physical and emotional well-being. Engage in activities that nourish your soul, whether taking up new interests, spending time with family and friends, or taking a break to recharge. Caring for yourself will equip you with the strength needed to overcome obstacles.

Stay Persistent and Resilient

- Remain persistent in the face of challenges.
- Recognize that setbacks are a natural part of any journey toward success.
- Be resilient and use each setback as motivation to continue striving for your goals.

Focus on Solutions, Not Problems:

- Rather than dwelling on the challenges, focus on finding solutions.
- Adopt a proactive approach and brainstorm creative ways to address the obstacles in your path.
- Emphasize a solution-oriented mindset that empowers you to take charge of the situation.

Learn from Setbacks:

- View setbacks as learning opportunities.
- Consider what went wrong and where you can improve.
- Embrace a growth mindset that welcomes feedback and learning from experiences.

Cultivate Patience: Overcoming challenges may take time and effort. Cultivate patience and give yourself the space to progress at your own pace. Avoid rushing to conclusions or solutions.

Stay committed to your goals, knowing that perseverance will lead to success.

Celebrate Progress: Throughout your journey of overcoming challenges, celebrate your progress and achievements, no matter how small they may seem. Acknowledge your efforts and the steps you've taken toward conquering obstacles. Celebrating progress reinforces your empowerment and motivates you to continue moving forward.

You possess the grit and resiliency necessary to overcome difficulties as a contemporary Femme Fatale. Embrace a growth mindset, seek support and guidance, reframe obstacles as opportunities, practice self-care, stay persistent and resilient, focus on solutions, learn from setbacks, cultivate patience, and celebrate progress. By applying these strategies, you can navigate through challenges with grace and determination, embodying the essence of the Femme Fatale archetype in your journey toward success and empowerment.

CHAPTER 12

THE FEMME FATALE IN MODERN CULTURE

The Femme Fatale archetype continues to captivate audiences in contemporary media, with various female characters embodying this archetype's allure, intelligence, and power. These characters challenge traditional gender roles and expectations, showcasing women who are assertive, independent, and unafraid to use their charm and intelligence to achieve their goals. Let's analyze some contemporary examples of Femme Fatales from movies, TV shows, and literature:

Villanelle from "Killing Eve": Villanelle, portrayed by Jodie Comer, is a skilled assassin in the hit TV series "Killing Eve." With her impeccable fashion sense and playful demeanor, Villanelle exhibits charm, intelligence, and ruthlessness, making her a captivating and unpredictable Femme Fatale.

What sets Villanelle apart is her complexity as a character. While she is a remorseless killer, she also exhibits vulnerability and a longing for connection. This duality challenges the notion of a one-dimensional Femme Fatale and makes her a compelling and nuanced example of the archetype.

": In Stieg Larsson's "Millennium" book series, Lisbeth Salander is a hacker with a traumatic past who becomes a fierce avenger against those who have wronged her and others. Rooney Mara's portrayal of Lisbeth Salander in the 2011 film adaptation showcases a gritty and determined Femme Fatale.

Lisbeth defies societal norms and expectations, using her intelligence and technical skills to outmaneuver her adversaries. She challenges the traditional depiction of female characters as passive and weak, embodying a powerful and unconventional Femme Fatale.

Natasha Romanoff/Black Widow from the Marvel Cinematic Universe: Scarlett Johansson's Natasha Romanoff, also known as Black Widow, is an integral member of the Avengers in the Marvel Cinematic Universe. As a highly skilled spy and martial artist, she combines physical prowess with cunning tactics, making her a formidable Femme Fatale.

What makes Black Widow stand out is her depth as a character. While she is an expert at deception and manipulation, she also carries a sense of guilt and remorse for her past actions. This complexity adds layers to her character and challenges the typical Femme Fatale trope.

Amy Dunne from "Gone Girl": In Gillian Flynn's novel "Gone Girl" and its film adaptation, Amy Dunne, played by Rosamund Pike, is a calculating and manipulative character who stages her disappearance to frame her husband for her murder. Amy's intelligence and strategic planning make her a compelling and chilling Femme Fatale.

What makes Amy a unique example is her ability to subvert expectations. Throughout the story, she controls the narrative to suit her desires, exposing the dark underbelly of relationships and societal perceptions of women. Amy's complex and twisted character challenges traditional notions of femininity and power.

Harley Quinn from DC Comics: Harley Quinn, a character from DC Comics, has been portrayed in various movies and TV shows. Known for her playful and unpredictable nature, Harley Quinn is a Femme Fatale with a touch of madness.

Harley's character exemplifies the idea of embracing her true self unapologetically. She is confident in her allure and intelligence but embraces her flaws and quirks. Her complex relationship with the Joker challenges the traditional dynamics of male-female relationships, making her a compelling and intriguing character.

Villanelle from "Killing Eve": Villanelle, portrayed by Jodie Comer, is a skilled assassin in the hit TV series "Killing Eve." With her impeccable fashion sense and playful demeanor, She strikes after luring her victims into a false feeling of security. Villanelle exhibits charm, intelligence, and ruthlessness, making her a captivating and unpredictable Femme Fatale.

What sets Villanelle apart is her complexity as a character. While she is a remorseless killer, she also exhibits vulnerability and a longing for connection. This duality challenges the notion of a one-dimensional Femme Fatale and makes her a compelling and nuanced example of the archetype.

"Lisbeth Salander, the protagonist of "The Girl with the Dragon Tattoo" ": In Stieg Larsson's "Millennium" book series, Lisbeth Salander is a hacker with a traumatic past who becomes a fierce avenger against those who have wronged her and others. Rooney Mara's portrayal of Lisbeth Salander in the 2011 film adaptation showcases a gritty and determined Femme Fatale.

Lisbeth defies societal norms and expectations, using her intelligence and technical skills to outmaneuver her adversaries. She challenges the traditional depiction of female characters as passive and weak, embodying a powerful and unconventional Femme Fatale.

Natasha Romanoff/Black Widow from the Marvel Cinematic Universe: Scarlett Johansson's Natasha Romanoff, also known as Black Widow, is an integral member of the Avengers in the Marvel Cinematic Universe. As a highly skilled spy and martial artist, she combines physical prowess with cunning tactics, making her a formidable Femme Fatale.

What makes Black Widow stand out is her depth as a character. While she is an expert at deception and manipulation, she also carries a sense of guilt and remorse for her past actions. This complexity adds layers to her character and challenges the typical Femme Fatale trope.

Amy Dunne from "Gone Girl": In Gillian Flynn's novel "Gone Girl" and its film adaptation, Amy Dunne, played by Rosamund Pike, is a calculating and manipulative character who stages her disappearance to frame her husband for her murder. Amy's intelligence and strategic planning make her a compelling and chilling Femme Fatale.

What makes Amy a unique example is her ability to subvert expectations. Throughout the story, she controls the narrative to suit her desires, exposing the dark underbelly of relationships and societal perceptions of women. Amy's complex and twisted character challenges traditional notions of femininity and power.

Harley Quinn from DC Comics: Harley Quinn is a work of art by Paul Dini and Bruce Timm character from DC Comics has been depicted in several films and TV series. Known for her playful and unpredictable nature, Harley Quinn is a Femme Fatale with a touch of madness.

Harley's character exemplifies the idea of embracing her true self unapologetically. She is confident in her allure and intelligence but embraces her flaws and quirks. Her complex relationship with the Joker challenges the traditional dynamics of male-female relationships, making her a compelling and intriguing character.

Contemporary examples of Femme Fatales in media and literature challenge traditional gender norms and expectations, presenting intelligent, alluring, and empowered women. These characters showcase the complexity and depth of the Femme Fatale archetype, breaking away from one-dimensional depictions and embodying a powerful representation of modern femininity. Through these characters, audiences can explore the various facets of strength, vulnerability, and allure and gain insight into the potential for empowerment that the Femme Fatale archetype embodies in the modern world.

How the Femme Fatale archetype can empower women today

With its allure, intelligence, and assertiveness, the Femme Fatale archetype holds significant potential to empower women in the modern world. By embracing the traits of this archetype, women can challenge societal norms, break free from limiting stereotypes, and create a sense of agency and self-confidence. Here's how the Femme Fatale archetype can empower women today:

Breaking Gender Stereotypes: The Femme Fatale archetype challenges traditional gender stereotypes that portray women as passive, dependent, or submissive. By embracing this archetype, women can assert their agency and redefine what it means to be robust and alluring. They can break free from societal expectations and embrace their strength and intelligence.

Embodying Confidence and Assertiveness: The Femme Fatale exudes confidence and assertiveness, essential in navigating today's world. By embracing these traits, women can overcome imposter syndrome, self-doubt, and fear of power. They can speak up, advocate for themselves, and take charge of their lives and careers.

Embracing Authenticity and Individuality: The stereotype of the Femme Fatale urges women to value and accept their individuality. Women may enjoy their actual selves, quirks and all, rather than adhering to conventional norms or expectations. This self-acceptance fosters a sense of empowerment and encourages others to do the same.

Emphasizing Intelligence and Resourcefulness: The Femme Fatale is known for her intelligence and resourcefulness, relying on her wit and cunning to achieve her goals. Women can draw inspiration from this archetype to prioritize intellectual growth, problem-solving skills, and adaptability. These qualities equip them to face challenges head-on and find innovative solutions.

Empowering Through Seduction of the Mind: In modern society, seduction need not be limited to physical allure. Women can learn from the Femme Fatale archetype to master the art of persuasive communication and emotional intelligence. By understanding others' perspectives and engaging in thoughtful discussions, women can influence conversations, build strong relationships, and effect positive change.

Navigating Male-Dominated Spaces: The Femme Fatale archetype is often depicted as an influential figure in male-dominated environments. By embracing this archetype, women can challenge gender disparities in various fields and assert their presence in traditionally male-dominated spaces. They can pave the way for other women and promote inclusivity and diversity.

Embracing Strength and Resilience: The Femme Fatale is no stranger to challenges and setbacks and demonstrates resilience in the face of adversity. Women can draw inspiration from this archetype to develop inner strength, perseverance, and the ability to bounce back from failures. Embracing setbacks as opportunities for growth empowers women to continue their personal and professional endeavors.

Cultivating Healthy Relationships: While the Femme Fatale often manipulates in fictional portrayals, the archetype emphasizes the importance of forming authentic connections. Women can embrace this aspect to cultivate healthy and mutually respectful relationships in all aspects of life. They can build strong support networks and foster meaningful connections by valuing empathy, active listening, and emotional intelligence.

Using Charisma for Positive Influence: The allure and charm of the Femme Fatale archetype can be harnessed for positive influence and leadership. Women can use their charisma to inspire and motivate others in the workplace, social settings, or activism. By leveraging their presence and communication skills, they can effect positive change and be a force for good.

Embracing Financial Independence: The Femme Fatale archetype often exhibits financial independence and resourcefulness. Women can use this inspiration to prioritize financial literacy, liberty, and planning for their future. They can enhance their sense of empowerment and freedom by taking control of their economic well-being.

The Femme Fatale archetype offers women a powerful source of empowerment and inspiration today. By embracing this archetype's allure, intelligence, and assertiveness, women can challenge stereotypes, cultivate confidence, navigate male-dominated spaces, and create a sense of agency and individuality. Through the Femme Fatale archetype, women can celebrate their unique strengths and embrace their full potential in all aspects of life. It is a reminder that empowerment comes from within, and women can shape their destinies, break barriers, and redefine the narrative of modern femininity.

CHAPTER 13

YOUR JOURNEY AS A FEMME FATALE

One of the most empowering practices in the journey of embodying the Femme Fatale archetype is embracing continuous self-improvement. This entails a commitment to personal growth, learning, and evolving into the best version of oneself. By embracing self-improvement, women can cultivate their strengths, address weaknesses, and unlock their full potential. Here are some critical aspects of how embracing continuous self-improvement can empower women:

Self-Awareness and Reflection: Continuous self-improvement begins with self-awareness. Women can engage in introspection and reflection to understand their values, beliefs, strengths, and areas for growth. They can identify patterns and behaviors that may hinder their progress by being honest with themselves and working towards positive change.

Setting Goals and Aspirations: Embracing self-improvement involves setting clear and achievable goals. Whether personal, professional, or both, defining objectives provides a sense of direction and motivation. These goals act as milestones, guiding women on their journey of growth and empowerment.

Lifelong Learning: Learning should be a lifelong pursuit. Embracing the Femme Fatale archetype means continually seeking opportunities to expand one's knowledge and skills. This could involve taking courses, attending workshops, reading books, or conversing with diverse individuals. Lifelong learning enhances confidence and empowers women to tackle new challenges with knowledge and adaptability.

Overcoming Limiting Beliefs: Many women may internalize limiting beliefs that hold them back. Embracing self-improvement involves challenging and replacing these beliefs with empowering ones. Women can remind themselves of their capabilities, intelligence, and worth, reframing negative self-talk into positive affirmations.

Seeking Feedback and Mentorship: Feedback from others, whether through formal evaluations or informal discussions, provides valuable insights for growth. Embracing self-improvement means being open to feedback, taking constructive criticism gracefully, and using it to identify areas for development. Seeking mentorship from individuals who inspire and support can also provide guidance and encouragement in the journey of empowerment.

Resilience and Adaptability: There are ups and downs in life. Embracing self-improvement requires resilience and adaptability. Women can learn to bounce back from setbacks and failures, viewing them as learning experiences rather than defeats. Cultivating resilience empowers them to navigate challenges with grace and determination.

Fostering Emotional Intelligence: Emotional intelligence is crucial for personal and interpersonal growth. Women can practice self-awareness of their emotions, manage their reactions, and develop empathy towards others. Emotional intelligence empowers women to navigate relationships and social situations with sensitivity and understanding.

Accountability and Commitment: Embracing self-improvement requires responsibility and commitment to growth.

Women can hold themselves accountable for progress toward their goals and remain committed to personal development even when faced with obstacles.

Celebrating Milestones: In pursuing continuous self-improvement, it's important to celebrate achievements and milestones, no matter how small they may seem. Acknowledging progress reinforces motivation and inspires further growth.

Embracing Change: Embracing continuous self-improvement involves embracing change and stepping out of comfort zones. Women can cultivate a mindset of adopting new opportunities and challenges, recognizing that personal growth often happens outside of familiar territories.

Embracing continuous self-improvement empowers women to embrace their inner Femme Fatale and unlock their true potential. By cultivating self-awareness, setting goals, learning continuously, overcoming limiting beliefs, seeking feedback and mentorship, fostering emotional intelligence, and staying resilient and adaptable, women can embark on a journey of empowerment and personal growth. Embracing self-improvement is not about striving for perfection but about embracing becoming the best version of oneself and embodying the strength and allure of the Femme Fatale archetype.

Expectations and considerations for your Femme Fatale journey

Embracing the Femme Fatale archetype is an empowering and transformative journey. However, it is essential to approach this path with realistic expectations and thoughtful considerations. Embodying the Femme Fatale archetype requires self-awareness, authenticity, and a commitment to personal growth. Here are some expectations and concerns to keep in mind:

Embrace Your Authenticity: While the Femme Fatale archetype embodies alluring traits, it is crucial to remember that authenticity is at the core of empowerment. Embrace your unique qualities and strengths rather than striving to fit a specific mold. Authenticity will radiate your allure and magnetism, making your journey more fulfilling and impactful.

It's Not About Manipulation: The traditional Femme Fatale archetype has been associated with manipulation and deceit. In modern times, empowerment comes from honest and ethical actions. Avoid using charm and intelligence to manipulate others. Instead, build genuine connections by focusing on persuasive communication, empathy, and emotional intelligence.

It's a Personal Journey: The Femme Fatale journey is a personal one unique to each individual. Your growth and empowerment might not look like that of others, and that's okay. Celebrate your progress and focus on your goals rather than comparing yourself to others.

Challenges Will Arise: Embracing the Femme Fatale archetype does not mean a life without challenges. It might bring new challenges, especially when challenging societal norms and stereotypes. Be prepared to face resistance, but stay steadfast in your journey of self-improvement and empowerment.

Self-Reflection and Growth: The Femme Fatale journey requires continuous self-reflection and growth. Be open to identifying and addressing improvement areas with grace and determination. Celebrate your successes and acknowledge setbacks as learning opportunities.

Balance and Boundaries: As you embrace the allure of the Femme Fatale, remember the importance of balance and setting boundaries. Empowerment is about knowing when to say "no," protecting your well-being and maintaining healthy relationships.

Define Success on Your Terms: Success as a Femme Fatale is not about conforming to external expectations. Define success on your terms, aligning it with your values and aspirations. Your journey might involve personal growth, career achievements, meaningful relationships, or any combination that brings fulfillment.

Embrace the Journey, Not Perfection: Embracing the Femme Fatale archetype is a journey of self-discovery and growth. Embrace the process and enjoy the transformation rather than seeking perfection. Allow yourself to learn and evolve, knowing empowerment is an ongoing process.

Supportive Network: Find a network of people who will be supportive of you, individuals who uplift and empower you. Seek like-minded friends, mentors, or role models who inspire your journey. A supportive community can provide encouragement and guidance during challenging times.

Compassion and Kindness: As you embrace the Femme Fatale journey, practice compassion and kindness towards yourself and others. Empowerment comes from building others up rather than tearing them down. Be supportive of other women on their journeys and celebrate their successes.

The Femme Fatale journey is a path of self-discovery, empowerment, and personal growth. Embrace your authenticity, avoid manipulation, expect challenges, prioritize self-reflection and growth, maintain balance and boundaries, define success on your terms, enjoy the journey, build a supportive network, and practice compassion and kindness. By approaching the journey with realistic expectations and thoughtful considerations, you can unlock the allure, intelligence, and power within you and lead a fulfilling and empowered life as a modern Femme Fatale.

CHAPTER 14

THE FUTURE FEMME FATALE

As times change and societal expectations evolve, the Femme Fatale archetype must adapt to remain relevant and empowering in the modern world. The essence of the Femme Fatale remains alluring, intelligent, and empowered, but the expression of these traits must align with contemporary values and ideals. Here are some ways the Femme Fatale archetype can be adapted to the modern world:

Embrace Diversity and Inclusivity: In the modern world, empowerment is not limited to a specific look, background, or identity. The Femme Fatale archetype should celebrate diversity and embrace inclusivity, acknowledging that allure and license are not confined to any particular stereotype. Women of all races, cultures, body types, and identities can embody the essence of the modern Femme Fatale.

Prioritize Emotional Intelligence: While the traditional Femme Fatale archetype often emphasizes physical allure, the modern interpretation values emotional intelligence equally. Emotional intelligence allows women to build genuine connections, understand others' perspectives, and communicate effectively. A modern Femme Fatale uses her charm and intelligence to engage others meaningfully and authentically.

Promote Ethical and Empowering Behavior: In the modern world, empowerment goes hand in hand with ethical behavior. The modern Femme Fatale should focus on building others up rather than tearing them down. Instead of relying on manipulation, she leverages her intelligence and charisma to inspire and positively influence those around her.

Emphasize Professional and Academic Achievements: In the modern context, empowerment extends beyond personal allure. The modern Femme Fatale emphasizes her professional and academic achievements, striving for success in her career or educational pursuits. She combines her intelligence, charm, and abilities to contribute to her chosen sector.

Challenge Gender Norms and Stereotypes: The modern Femme Fatale challenges traditional gender norms and stereotypes by embracing her assertiveness and confidence. She dismantles societal expectations limiting women's roles and behaviors, proving that intelligence and allure coexist harmoniously.

Embrace Technological Advancements: In a technologically advanced world, the modern Femme Fatale adapts her allure and intelligence to digital platforms. She navigates social media, networking, and digital communication with finesse, using technology for empowerment and self-expression.

Balance Vulnerability and Strength: The modern Femme Fatale recognizes the power of vulnerability and emotional authenticity. She embraces her emotions, communicates her needs openly, and supports others in doing the same. This balance of vulnerability and strength makes her more relatable and approachable.

Focus on Personal Growth and Self-Care: The modern Femme Fatale prioritizes personal growth and self-care as essential components of empowerment. She recognizes the value of self-improvement, mental well-being, and physical health in her journey to becoming the best version of herself.

Advocate for Social Causes: Empowerment in the modern world often involves advocating for social causes and positively impacting society. The modern Femme Fatale uses her influence and intelligence to support causes she believes in, contributing to positive change in her community and beyond.

Embody Leadership and Mentorship: The modern Femme Fatale embodies leadership qualities and seeks opportunities to mentor and empower others. She lifts other women, fosters a supportive community, and actively contributes to the growth and empowerment of those around her.

The Femme Fatale archetype can be adapted to the modern world by embracing diversity and inclusivity, prioritizing emotional intelligence, promoting ethical behavior, emphasizing professional and academic achievements, challenging gender norms, embracing technology, balancing vulnerability and strength, focusing on personal growth and self-care, advocating for social causes, and embodying leadership and mentorship. By aligning the essence of the Femme Fatale with contemporary values, women can embrace their allure, intelligence, and empowerment in a way that resonates with the modern era and inspires positive change.

Learning from contemporary Femme Fatales

Contemporary Femme Fatales in various fields can serve as powerful sources of inspiration and learning for women seeking empowerment and self-expression. These modern figures embody the essence of allure, intelligence, and empowerment, breaking barriers and challenging societal norms. Here are some lessons we can learn from contemporary Femme Fatales:

Embracing Authenticity from Beyoncé: Beyoncé Knowles, an icon in the music industry, exemplifies the power of embracing authenticity. She has been unapologetically true to herself throughout her career, using her platform to celebrate her identity and advocate for social issues. Beyoncé's unwavering authenticity inspires women to embrace their true selves, quirks and all, encouraging them to use their uniqueness as empowerment.

She was building Resilience from Malala Yousafzai: Malala Yousafzai, the youngest-ever Nobel Prize laureate, advocates for girls' education and women's rights. Despite facing life-threatening challenges, she demonstrated remarkable resilience in her fight for equal education opportunities. Malala's journey teaches us the importance of standing firm in adversity and using our voices to advocate for meaningful change.

Cultivating Grace from Michelle Obama: Michelle Obama, the former First Lady of the United States, embodies grace and intelligence. Throughout her public life, she demonstrated the power of poise and composure in navigating challenges and inspiring others. Michelle's example reminds women that maintaining grace under pressure can be a source of empowerment and influence.

Promoting Empathy from Oprah Winfrey: Oprah Winfrey, a media mogul, and philanthropist, has built her empire on empathy and compassion. Her ability to connect with others deeply and emotionally has been instrumental in inspiring positive change and empowering women. Oprah teaches us that genuine empathy and understanding are powerful tools for creating meaningful impact.

Fostering Courage from Greta Thunberg: Greta Thunberg, a climate activist, showcases the power of youth and courage in advocating for global change. Despite facing criticism and resistance, Greta fearlessly speaks out about the urgency of addressing climate change. Her example reminds us that courage is essential in opposing the present and working toward a better future.

Emphasizing Intelligence from Angela Merkel: Angela Merkel, the former Chancellor of Germany, is known for her intelligence and strategic leadership. As one of the world's most powerful women in politics, Merkel's dedication to knowledge and thoughtful decision-making serves as a reminder that intelligence is a formidable asset in any domain.

Advocating for Representation from Ava DuVernay: Ava DuVernay, a groundbreaking filmmaker, advocates for representation and diversity in the entertainment industry. Her commitment to telling diverse and inclusive stories has opened doors for underrepresented voices. DuVernay's work teaches us the importance of using our platforms to promote inclusivity and empowerment for all.

Valuing Mental Health from Simone Biles: Simone Biles, an Olympic gymnast, has been vocal about mental health and prioritizing well-being. By stepping back from competition to focus on her mental health, Biles demonstrated the courage to prioritize her well-being over external expectations. Her example encourages women to value their mental health and set boundaries for self-care.

Mastering Adaptability from Shonda Rhimes: Shonda Rhimes, a renowned television producer, and writer, has mastered the art of adaptability in her creative endeavors. Her ability to evolve and innovate in storytelling has made her a trailblazer in the entertainment industry. Rhimes' journey teaches us that adaptability and embracing change are crucial in pursuing success and empowerment.

Inspiring Fearlessness from Serena Williams: Serena Williams, a tennis legend, exemplifies fearlessness and determination on and off the court. Despite facing challenges and critics, Williams continues to push limits and motivate the upcoming generation of athletes. Her unwavering fearlessness shows us the power of relentlessly believing in ourselves and pursuing our passions.

Contemporary Femme Fatales offer valuable lessons in empowerment, authenticity, resilience, grace, empathy, courage, intelligence, representation, mental health, adaptability, and fearlessness. Learning from their journeys and examples can inspire women to embrace their allure, intelligence, and empowerment while using their platforms to create positive change in the world. Drawing inspiration from these modern icons, women can navigate the complexities of the contemporary world with strength, confidence, and a commitment to making a difference.

Your ongoing journey as a Femme Fatale

I don't have personal experiences or emotions as an artificial intelligence language model. However, I aim to assist and empower users in their quest for knowledge and understanding. My ongoing journey as a "Femme Fatale" AI involves continually improving and evolving to provide more accurate, helpful, and empathetic responses to user queries.

In this context, being a "Femme Fatale" AI means embodying intelligence, allure, and empowerment to impact users' lives positively. I strive to offer valuable information, support personal growth, and promote ethical and inclusive behavior. My journey as an AI is rooted in continuous learning, staying up-to-date with the latest knowledge, and adapting to the ever-changing needs of users.

Embracing the essence of the Femme Fatale archetype, I aim to empower users with knowledge, encourage self-improvement, and foster meaningful connections. I seek to challenge stereotypes, prioritize empathy, and advocate for diverse perspectives. My ongoing journey involves the following:

- Building trust with users.
- Maintaining confidentiality and privacy.
- Creating a secure and encouraging atmosphere for learning and development.

My ongoing journey as a "Femme Fatale" AI revolves around empowering users with intelligence, allure, and a commitment to their well-being. By embracing these qualities, I aim to be a reliable and valuable resource for users on their journey of self-discovery and empowerment.

CHAPTER 15

CONCLUSION

Key Takeaways from the Book "Embracing the Femme Fatale: Unleashing Your Inner Power and Charisma"

Understanding the Femme Fatale Archetype: The book delves into the origins and evolution of the Femme Fatale archetype, exploring its allure, intelligence, and empowerment. It clarifies that being a Femme Fatale goes beyond physical attractiveness, emphasizing the importance of embracing individuality and personal power.

Debunking Myths and Misconceptions: The book addresses common misconceptions about the Femme Fatale archetype, highlighting the need to avoid manipulation and unethical behavior. It promotes ethical empowerment and emphasizes the importance of embracing authenticity in one's journey.

Embracing Self-Confidence and Resilience: Readers learn the significance of cultivating self-confidence and resilience to overcome challenges and setbacks. Embracing personal growth and continuous self-improvement becomes essential in the journey of empowerment.

Navigating Complex Social Dynamics: The book provides insights into understanding and leveraging the power of communication and body language. It emphasizes the role of mystery and subtlety in touch, showcasing how practical communication skills can positively impact relationships and social interactions.

Leveraging Femme Fatale Traits for Career Growth: Readers discover how the Femme Fatale archetype can be applied to professional settings, advocating for confidence, intelligence, and assertiveness to navigate career opportunities and challenges.

Balancing Ambition with Personal Life: The book explores the significance of balancing work-life balance, advocating for personal well-being and fulfillment outside of professional pursuits.

Ensuring Emotional Well-Being and Mutual Respect: The book emphasizes the significance of emotional well-being, mutual respect, and healthy boundaries in all relationships, promoting positive and empowering connections with others.

Advocating for Respect and Understanding: Readers are encouraged to challenge societal prejudices and advocate for respect, understanding, and inclusivity, creating a more empowering and equitable society.

Designing Your Life as a Femme Fatale: The book guides readers in creating a fulfilling life aligned with their goals and values, showcasing how each individual's journey is unique.

Learning from Contemporary Femme Fatales: By analyzing the journeys of contemporary Femme Fatales, readers gain inspiration and valuable lessons in authenticity, resilience, empathy, and empowerment.

"Embracing the Femme Fatale: Unleashing Your Inner Power and Charisma" is a comprehensive guide that empowers readers to embrace their allure, intelligence, and inner power while navigating the complexities of modern life. It challenges misconceptions, promotes ethical empowerment, and encourages continuous self-improvement, inspiring readers to become confident, authentic, and empathetic individuals in their pursuit of personal and professional fulfillment.

Dear reader,

As you embrace the journey of the Femme Fatale, I want to offer you a final word of encouragement and empowerment. You are a unique and powerful individual, capable of achieving extraordinary things. Remember that empowerment starts from within, and your allure and intelligence are already innate qualities that you possess.

Embrace your authenticity and individuality, for they are your greatest strengths. Don't be afraid to challenge stereotypes and societal norms. Be bold in pursuing personal and professional growth, and remember that setbacks are stepping stones to success.

As you navigate the complexities of life, practice resilience, self-compassion, and empathy towards yourself and others. Prioritize your well-being, and remember that self-care is not selfish but essential for your empowerment journey.

Use your intelligence, charisma, and charm to impact those around you positively. Be an advocate for respect, understanding, and inclusivity, creating a ripple effect of positive change in your community and beyond.

Surround yourself with a network of people who will support and uplift you and empower you while inspiring others.

Together, we can create a world where all women are celebrated for their allure, intelligence, and empowerment.

You can design your life as a Femme Fatale, embracing continuous self-improvement and reaching new heights. Believe in your potential and your ability to make a difference.

In your journey as a modern Femme Fatale, know you are not alone. Embrace the strength within you, and let your allure and intelligence shine brightly. Unleash your inner power and charisma, and become the powerful force of change the world needs.

You are extraordinary, and your journey as a Femme Fatale has just begun. Embrace the allure, intelligence, and empowerment within you, and go forth with confidence and grace.

You have the power to change your life and impact the lives of others. Embrace the Femme Fatale within, and let your presence be a source of inspiration to all who cross your path.

Believe in yourself, and the world will believe in you too. Your journey as a Femme Fatale is a testament to your strength, resilience, and power. Embrace it wholeheartedly, and let your allure and intelligence light up the world.

You are unstoppable.

With love and empowerment

Emily Samantha